IN THE WORDS OF

E. B. WHITE

IN THE WORDS OF

E. B. WHITE

*Quotations from America's Most
Companionable of Writers*

EDITED BY MARTHA WHITE

CORNELL UNIVERSITY PRESS

ITHACA AND LONDON

First published 2011 by Cornell University Press

Printed in the United States of America

Library of Congress Cataloging-in-Publication Data

White, E. B. (Elwyn Brooks), 1899–1985.
    In the words of E.B. White : quotations from America's most companionable of writers / edited by Martha White.
        p. cm.
    Includes bibliographical references and index.
    ISBN 978-0-8014-4955-0 (cloth : alk. paper)
    I. White, E. B. (Elwyn Brooks), 1899–1985—Quotations.   I. White, Martha, 1954 Dec. 18–   II. Title.
    PS3545.H5187A6   2011
    813'.52—dc22   2011021225

Cloth printing   10 9 8 7 6 5 4 3 2 I

FOR JOEL AND ALLENE WHITE, WITH LOVE,

EACH OF THEM LITERARY EXECUTORS BEFORE ME,

AND WHO TAUGHT ME EVERYTHING

I NEEDED TO KNOW.

CONTENTS

CONTENTS

CONTENTS

A NOTE TO THE READER

If I were to begin this note with one of White's signature *New Yorker* Newsbreak headings, it might be the "It's about Time Department" or possibly "Sentences We Hated to Come to the End Of." *In the Words of E. B. White* has allowed me an enjoyable year of reading back through his work. Dorothy Lobrano Guth (editor of the first edition of *The Letters of E. B. White*) had it right when she commented in 2005, "your grandfather never wrote a dull letter in his life."

That both editions of his letters are now on searchable discs has made this project that much easier. Most of E. B. White's letters and papers reside at the Carl A. Kroch Library of Cornell University; my special thanks go to Katharine Reagan and her able associates, who have been invaluable help. I also owe a debt of gratitude to Katherine Romans Hall, who compiled *E. B. White, A Bibliographic Catalogue of Printed Materials in the Department of Rare Books, Cornell University Library,* 1979. Hall's book helped me to supply dates to many essays and poems. Likewise, the 1925–2005 (and updates) of *The Complete New Yorker* on CDs enabled me to search the magazine archives for E. B. White's work and quickly find anything among his contributions. (Call this the "Neatest Trick of the Week.")

For the task of selecting quotations and categories, I reflected first on some common themes in his essays including time, democracy, style, the country, and the city. The many permissions requests we field for reprints of his work gave me a sense of what has remained popular and current. Rereading E. B. White's body of work, once again, allowed some of his best and most memorable expressions to resurface, and I was struck by their timelessness. My father, Joel, had done a similarly comprehensive rereading when he spent an hour a night reading aloud to my grandfather, who was increasingly bedridden during his last year. Many of their favorites were recorded by my father on *White on White*, an audio version of some of the essays, so I have culled from those, especially, as among the best of the best.

In many cases, multiple categories could have been assigned, so I have been whimsical at times. I trust the index and cross-references will lead readers where they want to go. I have weeded for redundancies, or where material seemed to lack current appeal. With dates, I have adopted one style, rather than the various ones (or the lack) that graced his book collections. The quotations are listed roughly chronologically, under their respective headings, except where I let thematic highlights dominate. As for spelling, few corrections were necessary. Stuart Little spoke for my grandfather when he said, "a misspelled word is an abomination in the sight of everyone." Any mistakes are my own.

In the matter of attributions, I have attempted to identify where the quotations originally appeared, and also included (where I could) the volume(s) in which individual quotations were reprinted, especially where those books remain in print today. Many of the quotations were published first in *The New Yorker*; however, as not everyone owns the hefty CD archive, I have identified the books where the quotations are reprinted. Remarkably, a quick Internet search shows dozens of E. B. White quotations on countless websites, but the sites rarely note the sources. Worse, many quotations are incorrectly attributed to White, inaccurately written or punctuated, or badly excerpted. (Newsbreak headline: "What Paper D'Ya Read?" but for *paper* substitute *website*—and let the reader beware.) I hope this book will prove an authoritative help to those who want to know what E. B. White *actually* wrote, and if and when he *in fact* wrote it. In some cases, accounting for the context provides insight into *why* E. B. White wrote what he did. I encourage you to seek out the original sources to read more of his words.

Ironically, some of you will stand at a podium and deliver White's pithy prose to punctuate speeches and oral presentations, an exercise that White avoided because of a lifelong fear of public speaking. (File this under his "Perish the Thought Department.") If this collection inspires you to read more of E. B. White, or think or speak or write more clearly yourself, then this work will have been worthwhile. Consider this my small entry for the "All's Right with the World Department."

IN THE WORDS OF

E. B. WHITE

INTRODUCTION

"A Simple and Sincere Account"

> I should not talk so much about myself if there
> were anybody else whom I knew as well....Moreover,
> on my side, I require of every writer, first or last,
> a simple and sincere account of his own life, and not
> merely what he has heard of other men's lives.
>
> —Henry David Thoreau, *Walden*

When I was born, my grandfather (1899–1985) was fifty-five, exactly my age when I finished this book project that has allowed me, for the second time, to spend a year reading through the greater part of his work. (The first time was when I was editing the revised edition of the *Letters of E. B. White* to include letters from the final decade of his life.) For years now, my office has been cluttered with the offshoots of *his* office: shelves of his books; boxes of Blackwing pencils; old family scrapbooks and photographs; and a wooden model of *Flounder*, the scow he built for my father, Joel, when he was ten. On the wall above my desk hangs a printed sheet from *The New Yorker*, titled "Newsbreak Department Heads," listing the headlines for the small fillers where typographical errors and bad writing were held up for amusement. His additions are penciled in: "Balderdash Department," "Constabulary

Notes from All Over," "No Vivid Writing, Please," and "Sentences We Hated to Come to the End Of," to name a few. For most of the three decades that he and I shared, however, I didn't think of him as E. B. White, or Andy, or even as a writer; I thought of him as Grandpa.

Don't Give It a Second Thought Department

We first met, or so I was told, when he produced the jackknife that cut my bonnet ribbons free from my sleeper-suit zipper on my way home from the hospital, a story that delighted him in the retelling. Later, he became my guide to his shore and barnyard and the heart-shaped skating pond in his meadow. For swimming, he gave me an inflatable frog named Greeno, who lived in his boatshed/writing studio on Allen Cove, and he once humored me by helping to rescue Greeno from the iced-in boatshed, far down a dirt road from the house, after a snowstorm. For all I knew, that emergency seemed just as real to him as it did to me. Years later, he loaned me a broody hen to finish incubating a clutch of duck eggs after their mother had died. We also shared a love of dogs. My grandfather loved sailing and spending time at my father's boatyard, where he had a small sloop built and named for me. He sailed the *Martha* well beyond the time when he felt comfortable on the water ("I cannot not sail," he wrote[1]), and the sloop can still be seen in the vicinity of Penobscot Bay, a pleasant reminder of both my father (her designer and builder) and my grandfather.

I was eight when he gave me a signed copy of *Stuart Little*, but I recall only the barest glimmer that he was its author. I preferred it to *Charlotte's Web*, because of Stuart's small size and love of skating, plus I was a realist and knew that the pigs and geese on my grandfather's farm ended up on our Sunday dinner table, not at the Blue Hill Fair. I read the hot-off-the-press *The Trumpet of the Swan* on my grandparents' living room couch, when I was home on holiday from boarding school. (The Brooklin, Maine high school had closed, with a final graduating class of two.)

My send-off gift for school, a copy of *The Elements of Style*, had been inscribed "and you can use all the needless words you want to," and my dawning awareness of who E. B. White *was* began about then. I met the news with mixed pride and disdain. When an occasional classmate would ask, too breathlessly, "What is your grandfather *like*?" I was apt to reply, "He's my grandfather. What is *your* grandfather like?"

One of my high school classes was reading James Thurber, at the time, which I must have reported, because I got this characteristic letter, in reply:

> If your American history course is based on Thurber's *My Life and Hard Times* it is probably the greatest distortion of history in history, but it must be a lot of fun. Oddly enough, I was reading the same book myself night before last, in preparation for the visit yesterday of Burton Bernstein, who is writing a biography of our old friend Jim Thurber. Burt is the brother of Leonard Bernstein and an awfully pleasant fellow. He had lunch with us (fried scallops) to pick our brains and our memories and spent part of the afternoon with us. Neither dog cared much for him....
>
> As a result of my American Book Committee award last week, my desk is piled higher than usual with unanswered letters. The N. Y. Times yesterday published my acceptance speech (delivered for me by William Maxwell)—with only two errors.[2]

If my letters had errors, they were sent back to me, red-penciled for my elucidation, but I was fortunate to know E. B. White first as a grandfather, and only later as a writer. What was clear to me, even as

3

E. B. White with granddaughter, Martha White, ca. 1956.

a child, was his unsurpassed capacity for wonder—at the first pullets'
eggs of the season, displayed in a black bowl in the living room; at the
antics of a series of small and often neurotic dogs; at a hummingbird
he'd had a chance to hold in his hand; and at the joys of grandchildren,
including here my younger brother:

> I had the ping pong table set up in the barn under a light, and
> this was a great success—with little John mounted on the milk-
> ing stool at one end and sometimes stretched out on his belly on
> the forecourt, in his great eagerness. I have never seen a 5-year
> old so determined to conquer every thing, every situation, every
> wall, and every body. He scales walls and other perpendicular
> surfaces with a kind of jet propulsion, supplied by his innards.[3]

Soon after he had first moved to Maine and built that wooden scow
for my father from plans in *The American Boy's Handybook*, White wrote:

> I think the best writing is often done by persons who are snatch-
> ing the time from something else—from an occupation, or
> from a profession, or from a jail term—something that is either
> burning them up, as religion, or love, or politics, or that is
> boring them to tears, as prison, or a brokerage house, or an
> advertising firm.[4]

The grandfather I knew, in his mid-career, had been bored to tears
at an advertising firm (one of his first jobs), but now snatched his
writing time primarily from farm chores. He kept chickens, sheep,
geese, sometimes Muscovy ducks, and he occasionally boarded other
people's cows. He built wheelbarrows, bookshelves, and dog crates,
and he rarely traveled to New York, anymore, relying instead on the
U.S. Mail to meet his deadlines. He was happy to be regarded as an

amateur farmer by his Maine neighbors and they guarded his privacy when someone came to visit the writer. As often as he could, he sailed or visited my father's boatyard to see what projects were underway. He came to our house to deliver eggs, check on my ducks or the dog we had adopted when he could no longer keep her, and he attended the Blue Hill Fair, where he loved the sheep dog trials and the livestock exhibits.

As his and my grandmother's health deteriorated, they spent occasional winters in Sarasota, Florida. There, he fished in the bayou, swam, fed (and named) the herons on the lawn, and visited the Ringling Bros. circus. He loved to watch the tents being set up or the early morning practice sessions of the performers. His essay "The Ring of Time"[5] was the working result of his keen observance of one such morning, and it became a family favorite, as well as a popular one. His sense of wonder is strong in that essay, and *that* is the grandfather—and only later, the writer—whom I knew. Another Florida essay—"What Do Our Hearts Treasure?"[6]—also depicts his sense of good fortune that we were lucky to share. My mother had sent a Christmas parcel to Sarasota, complete with balsam fir boughs and small gifts. As he described it, "The branch had unquestionably been whacked from a tree in the woods behind our son's house in Maine and had made the long trip south. It wore the look and carried the smell of authenticity. 'There!' said my wife, as though she had just delivered a baby." The box also held our small, homemade ornaments—paper drums with Q-tip drumsticks. "And the package contained school photographs, which we eagerly studied. Our youngest grandson had done something odd with his mouth, in a manly attempt to defeat the photographer, and looked just like Jimmy Hoffa. 'How marvelous! said my wife.'"[7]

The essay echoed the stuff of his letters home, so I didn't give it a second thought. Nearly half a century later, though, I know exactly which school photograph of my brother he was describing, because my brother *did* look just like Jimmy Hoffa in that shot. I remember the paper drums nestled in the balsam fir and I understand that Christmas in Florida suddenly seemed possible to my grandmother, who had been missing New England. My grandfather's extraordinary gift, first as a human being and second as a writer, was that he could retain and summon that lifelong sense of wonder and render it perfectly into words, to share not only his acute observation, but the great feeling (and often humor) attached. That's one for the Hoopla Department, in my opinion—but then, I am his granddaughter first.

O Pioneers! Department

Elwyn Brooks White was a letter writer and daily journal keeper from the age of eight or nine. As the youngest of the six children of Jessie Hart and Samuel Tilly White, Elwyn had been taught to read by his brother, Stanley, "a born teacher" who also taught his younger brother to paddle a canoe, use a jackknife (which I would later appreciate), and to follow both of his brothers to Cornell University.

> I could read fairly fluently when I entered the first grade—an accomplishment my classmates found annoying. I'm not sure my teacher, Miss Hackett, thought much of it, either. Stan's method of teaching me was to hand me a copy of the *New York Times* and show me how to sound the syllables. He assured me there was nothing to learning to read—a simple matter.[8]

When White was nine, he mentioned writing "a poem about a little mouse"[9] and also composing music. The *Woman's Home Companion* gave him a prize for the poem, and *St. Nicholas Magazine* soon awarded him two more, both for prose. Later, White wrote for his high school

E. B. White with calf, Mount Vernon, New York, very early 1900s.
Courtesy of the Division of Rare and Manuscript Collections,
Cornell University Library.

Oracle, in Mount Vernon, New York. At college, he earned the nickname "Andy" after Cornell's president Andrew D. White, earned two hard-won A's in Professor Strunk's advanced writing course in his junior year (where he would first encounter "the little book") and became editor-in-chief of the *Cornell Daily Sun,* in 1920. About then, young Andy White began contributing to Franklin Pierce Adams's prestigious column in the *New York World,* called "The Conning Tower." White recalled those early days of freelancing, saying, "One wrote for the sheer glory of it. Such times are unforgettable. If you were skilled in French verse forms, you could even make love to your girl in full view of a carload of subway riders who held the right newspaper opened to the right page. It was a fine era."[10]

When Andy White entered the work force, President Harding had inherited a serious recession and unemployment was rising. Today, we hear about the "Roaring Twenties," but it wasn't until 1923 that better times began. In the meantime, White was pounding the pavement in Manhattan and being turned away by various newspapers. Finally, he accepted a position feeding news wires for the United Press. Speed was everything, however, and he felt unsuited for it, so he quit within a week. Reluctantly, he became an ad man and continued sending love poems and other verse to "The Conning Tower." They accepted almost everything he submitted, but didn't pay a dime.

In the spring of 1922, restless and discouraged, he quit New York City to take a cross-country trip in his Model T Ford, Hotspur, with a former Cornell classmate, Howard Cushman. They funded the trip by their freelance efforts, including White's sonnet for a Kentucky Derby horse, his prize-winning limerick, and by hocking their typewriters. To make ends meet, they also sold roach powder, played the piano or cigar-box fiddle in cafes, sandpapered a dance floor, washed dishes, and ran a carnival concession. On the West Coast, they sought newspaper jobs, but Cushman soon gave up and went home. White became

E. B. White, probably at Cornell, 1919 or so.

a journalist and, briefly, a columnist for the *Seattle Times*. He was let go after some months, releasing him to board the *S. S. Buford* for a cruise to Alaska, along the Aleutians and on to Siberia. His essay "The Years of Wonder" recalls that time.[11] He paid his way there, then worked on the ship for his return passage to Seattle, where he sold his car and bought a train ticket home.

Returning to New York led to another ad job and a pay cut. White continued freelancing, mining his journals for material, and he placed a sonnet in "The Bowling Green" column in the *New York Evening Post*,[12] where it garnered an award. "The Conning Tower" continued to publish his work, as well as that of many of the names that would later appear in *The New Yorker*, then in its earliest inception.

Harold Ross's first issue appeared on February 19, 1925. Nine weeks later, and not quite twenty-six years old, E. B. White found his entry onto *The New Yorker*'s pages, writing about what he then knew best: advertising. A satire of automobile advertisements of the day, "A Step Forward," was run with his initials at the bottom. His first sentence began: "The advertising man takes over the VERNAL account" and the spoof continued: "Into every one of this season's song sparrows has been built the famous VERNAL tone. Look for the distinguishing white mark on the breast."[13]

White's second *New Yorker* piece, an essay, "Defense of the Bronx River,"[14] appeared in early May, and was followed by several more that year, a variety of light essays, fiction, and poetry. By mid-1926, he had been invited to drop in at the offices of *The New Yorker*. When he did so, it was editor Katharine S. Angell who met him. Years later, in the introduction to his book of *Letters*, White recalled their first meeting: "I sat there peacefully gazing at the classic features of my future wife without, as usual, knowing what I was doing."[15]

In those early years at *The New Yorker*, White not only fell in love with Katharine, but found his voice, polished his style, and began to make his fortune. Before long, he was setting the tone and style for the short paragraphs that made up the casual "Notes and Comment" in the front of the magazine. As he wrote to his brother Stanley, after the publication of his poetry collection *The Lady Is Cold:*

> I discovered a long time ago that writing of the small things of the day, the trivial matters of the heart, the inconsequential but near things of this living, was the only kind of creative work which I could accomplish with any sincerity or grace. As a reporter, I was a flop, because I always came back laden not with facts about the case, but with a mind full of the little difficulties and amusements I had encountered in my travels. Not till *The New Yorker* came along did I ever find any means of expressing those impertinences and irrelevancies. Thus yesterday, setting out to get a story on how police horses are trained, I ended by writing a story entitled "How Police Horses Are Trained" which never even mentions a police horse, but has to do entirely with my own absurd adventures at police headquarters. The rewards of such endeavor are not that I have acquired an audience or a following, as you suggest (fame of any kind being a Pyrrhic victory), but that sometimes in writing of myself— which is the only subject anyone knows intimately—I have occasionally had the exquisite thrill of putting my finger on a little capsule of truth, and heard it give the faint squeak of mortality under my pressure, an antic sound.[16]

Harold Ross knew better than to confine White to an office chair, but let him come and go, writing "Notes and Comment" for the Talk of the Town section, and editing taglines for the humorous "newsbreaks" that ran at the bottom of the page. White continued to submit poems and fiction, contributed occasional cartoon captions, and even painted

NEWSBREAK DEPARTMENT HEADS

ALL'S RIGHT WITH THE WORLD DEPARTMENT

ANSWERS TO HARD QUESTIONS

ANTICLIMAX DEPARTMENT

A THOUGHT FOR THIS WEEK
Balderdash Department
BLOCK THAT METAPHOR!

BRAVE NEW WORLD DEPARTMENT

BROTHERHOOD OF MAN DEPT.

CLEAR DAYS ON THE POLITICAL SCENE
Constabulary Notes from all over
DEPARTMENT OF BELLES-LETTRES

DEPARTMENT OF DELICACY

DEPARTMENT OF ELEGANCE

DEPT. OF ENGLISH LITERATURE

DEPT. OF HIGHER EDUCATION

DEPT. OF STRAIGHT THINKING

DEPT. OF UNDERSTATEMENT

DEPT. OF UTTER CONFUSION

DON'T GIVE IT A SECOND THOUGHT DEPARTMENT

FULLER EXPLANATION DEPT.

FUNNY COINCIDENCE DEPARTMENT

GO CLIMB A TREE DEPARTMENT

HIGHER MATHEMATICS DEPT.

HO-HUM DEPARTMENT

HOOPLA DEPARTMENT

HOW'S THAT AGAIN? DEPARTMENT

INFATUATION WITH SOUND OF OWN WORDS DEPARTMENT

IT'S ABOUT TIME DEPARTMENT

[LAUGHTER] ON CAPITOL HILL

LETTERS WE NEVER FINISHED READING

LIFE IN HOLLYWOOD DEPARTMENT

LOVE IS A WONDERFUL THING DEPARTMENT

MOST FASCINATING NEWS STORY OF THE WEEK

MR. CARLYLE, MEET MR. EMERSON

NEATEST TRICK OF THE WEEK

NO COMMENT DEPARTMENT

NON-SEQUITUR DEPARTMENT

NON-STOP SENTENCE DERBY
No Vivid Writing, Please
NO SOONER SAID THAN DONE DEPT.

ONCE A LADY ALWAYS A LADY DEPARTMENT

ONE WORLD DEPARTMENT

O PIONEERS DEPARTMENT

OUR FORGETFUL AUTHORS

OUR HUNGRY CRITICS

OUR OWN BUSINESS DIRECTORY

PERISH THE THOUGHT DEPT.

POESY DEPARTMENT

PROSE PASSAGES WE HATED TO COME TO THE END OF

PSHAW DEPARTMENT

PYRRHIC VICTORY DEPARTMENT

RAISED EYEBROWS DEPARTMENT

REMARKABLE REMARKS

REMARKS WE DOUBT EVER GOT MADE

RICH, BEAUTIFUL PROSE DEPT.

Sentences We Hated to Come to the End Of

RIP VAN WINKLE DEPARTMENT

SILVER LINING DEPARTMENT

SLIGHT HEADACHE DEPARTMENT

SOCIAL NOTES FROM ALL OVER

STATISTICAL DEPARTMENT

TCH, TCH DEPARTMENT

THAT'S TOO BAD DEPARTMENT

THE BUREAUCRATIC MIND AT WORK

THE CLOUDED CRYSTAL BALL

THE CREATIVE LIFE

THE GOOD OLD DAYS

THE LEGAL MIND AT WORK

THE LITERARY LIFE

THE LYRICAL PRESS

THE MYSTERIOUS EAST

THE NEW ARMY

THE PUBLISHING LIFE

THERE'LL ALWAYS BE AN ADMAN

THERE'LL ALWAYS BE AN ENGLAND

THIS CHANGING WORLD

THIS IS WAR

UH-HUH DEPARTMENT

UP LIFE'S LADDER

WE DON'T WANT TO HEAR ABOUT IT DEPARTMENT

WHAT PAPER D'YA READ?

WIND ON CAPITOL HILL DEPT.

WORDS OF ONE SYLLABLE DEPT.

SENTENCES WE LOST INTEREST IN BEFORE GETTING VERY FAR

NEWSBREAKS Department Headlines, with E. B. White's handwritten additions.

a cover,[17] a seahorse wearing a feed bag. His Newsbreak Department Heads included "Answers to Hard Questions," "Department of Utter Confusion," the "Ho-Hum Department" and "Sentences We Lost Interest in Before Getting Very Far." Their popularity led to two book collections of newsbreaks, *Ho-Hum* and *Another Ho-Hum.*

Early on, White shared an office—and a sense of humor—with writer and cartoonist James Thurber. By 1929, they had collaborated on their first book, a parody of sex manuals of the time, called *Is Sex*

E. B. White and James Thurber in New York City
(at the Algonquin?), ca. 1950s.

Necessary? and containing Thurber's illustrations. Thurber's prolific pencil drawings littered their office floor and waste bin, and it was White who first submitted one as a potential *New Yorker* cover, having colored it in without Thurber's prior knowledge.

The Creative Life

In the late 1930s, White began to chafe at the restrictions of urban life in New York and the constancy of his weekly deadlines. He and Katharine had begun vacationing in Maine with their son Joel and, in 1933, they bought a forty-acre salt water farm and began spending longer periods of time there. Four years later, White attempted what he called "My Year,"[18] a leave-of-absence from *The New Yorker* (and from his family) so he could remain in Maine to work on a sustained piece of writing. It didn't come off. By 1938, however, he had convinced his wife to abandon her much-loved editorial job for one handled through the mail, and they moved north.

Andy White continued to write comments, newsbreaks, and other work for *The New Yorker*, but according to his schedule, not theirs. He had turned down an editorship of the *Saturday Review*, and was working intermittently on *Stuart Little*. Just as he left New York, White traded his weekly deadlines for monthly ones, this time with *Harper's* magazine, beginning the "One Man's Meat" columns (1937–1941) that would become the basis for his most celebrated book of essays. In a later edition of that book, he described this time:

> Once in everyone's life there is apt to be a period when he is fully awake, instead of half asleep. I think of those five years in Maine as the time when this happened to me. Confronted by new challenges, surrounded by new acquaintances—including

E. B. White's stepson Roger Angell and son
Joel McCoun White, about 1940.

The Whites' house and barn (under the cupola) in North Brooklin, Maine.

the characters in the barnyard, who were later to reappear in *Charlotte's Web*—I was suddenly seeing, feeling, and listening as a child sees, feels, and listens. It was one of those rare interludes that can never be repeated, a time of enchantment. I am fortunate indeed to have had the chance to get some of it down on paper.[19]

White's career had begun to shift, from the urban-based casuals and editorial writing to his celebrated columns about country life. Over a decade of writing "Notes and Comment" in the editorial "we" was wearing thin, and White was ready to trade the uneasy anonymity of the plural pronoun for the unapologetic "I" of the personal essay. Life in Maine rekindled his sense of wonder, a "time of enchantment" when he was learning to farm, and it was here that he hit his stride and perfected the casual essay. He not only wrote about the farm, the coon tree, his dogs, Maine neighbors, and Hurricane Edna, but he was weaving in the larger themes of freedom, democracy, war and peace, religion and security, and the circle of time. Meanwhile, his voice (and others') continued to set the tone at *The New Yorker*, where he was already a renowned essayist and political commentator.

At about the same time, E. B. and Katharine White were collaborating on a collection of humor pieces, their nod to the war years, when humor seemed to lighten the load of daily discouraging news. *The Subtreasury of American Humor* appeared in 1941, with his comments on the under-appreciated role of humor in the American literary tradition. As if this were not enough, White was polishing up the first of his children's books. *Stuart Little* was published in 1945, selling over 100,000 copies in its first year, and *Charlotte's Web* appeared for the Christmas season in 1952, going almost immediately into a second printing. Jean Stafford wrote White to say, "I think I will commit the entire of it to memory,"[20] and Eudora Welty's review in the *New York Times Book Review* said: "As a piece of work it is just about perfect."[21]

E. B. White and his wife Katharine, taking a break from collaborating on *A Subtreasury of American Humor,* ca. 1940. Courtesy of the Division of Rare and Manuscript Collections, Cornell University Library.

With the appearance of *One Man's Meat* in book form in 1942, E. B. White was beginning to be "credited with restoring the informal essay to a place of respect."[22] Not infrequently, he was compared with Michel de Montaigne, whom he certainly read and emulated, Ralph Waldo Emerson, or other transcendentalists. Diana Trilling, reviewing *One Man's Meat* for the *Nation* said, "The kinship with Thoreau is explicit throughout the book but there is also Mr. White's implicit kinship with Montaigne."[23] William Soskin, reviewing *Every Day Is Saturday,* called him "The Perfect Modern Skeptic," and compared him to "The Pepysian man, the Montaigne man, the gentle ironist and the genuine Pyrrhonian" and credited White with "a sweet gift for the

E. B. White and Katharine, feeding the sheep in Maine, ca. 1940s.

precise and nice phrase."[24] White was more self-effacing, claiming: "it is more as though I were talking to myself while shaving."[25]

Certainly, White was playing with similar themes of the individual and his interdependence with other individuals, and the moral underpinnings of democracy, liberty, and justice. Although he regularly struck the moral note, he steered clear of denominational religious beliefs in his writing. By his own admission, White was primarily influenced by Henry David Thoreau and he wrote about him repeatedly.

Walden is the only book I own, although there are some others unclaimed on my shelves. Every man, I think, reads one book in his life, and this is mine. It is not the best book I ever encountered, perhaps, but it is for me the handiest, and I keep it about me in much the same way one carries a handkerchief—for relief in moments of defluxion or despair.[26]

He celebrated Thoreau's birth, death, and publishing anniversaries; he spoofed the Thoreau Society for trying to buy "the house at 73 Main Street, Concord, where Henry David Thoreau sat taking pot shots at the whole theory of shelter";[27] and he imitated him, comparing his own boat house and writing studio to Thoreau's place on Walden Pond.[28] He even used him as a literary device to speak up against Senator Joseph McCarthy's diatribes against suspected "un-American activities."[29] White considered Thoreau a writer, more than a naturalist or hermit, and he especially admired his ability to "name eighteen chapters by the use of only thirty-nine words," demonstrating "how sweet are the uses of brevity."[30] White had not forgotten Professor Strunk's "omit needless words," and after two decades of writing short paragraphs for *The New Yorker*, he had turned it into an art form. His office mate, James Thurber, declared that "No one can write a sentence like White,"[31] though many (including Thurber) sometimes tried, especially once the Whites left for Maine and the war years reduced the staff.

Department of English Literature

I can attest that White had many more books in his library than just *Walden*, but it was true that he didn't consider himself a reader or a literary man. He loved Clarence Day, Mark Twain, S. J. Perelman, Rachel Carson, and others, and he kept up with the newspapers. But he was, by his own admission, a slow reader and one who would rather be doing something else, whether building a wheel barrow or writing. In "Here Is New York," he said:

> I've been remembering what it felt like as a young man to live in the same town with giants. When I first arrived in New York my personal giants were a dozen or so columnists and critics and poets whose names appeared regularly in the papers. I burned with a low steady fever just because I was on the same island with Don Marquis, Heywood Broun, Christopher Morley, Franklin P. Adams, Robert C. Benchley, Frank Sullivan, Dorothy Parker, Alexander Woollcott, Ring Lardner and Stephen Vincent Benét.[32]

With almost equal measure, however, he loved dictionaries, consulting them often, and he enjoyed giving them, as on the occasion of a new baby. He read farm manuals, poultry guides, bird books, and nautical charts, and was more apt to write about these than anything on the literary scene. He refused to write book blurbs or name favorites, and he rarely wrote an introduction or foreword to a book, two notable exceptions being one he penned for Don Marquis and another for a poultry guide.

Andy White read Ernest Hemingway just enough to parody him. His essay "Across the Street and Into the Grill"[33] poked fun "with my respects" at one of the few writers whose style was considered as spare and as distinctly American as White's—though, they couldn't have been more different, in their writing styles or in their politics. (No one ever called "Papa" Hemingway self-deprecating.) While Hemingway was in Europe writing about Spanish bullfighters, ambulance drivers, and ex-patriots, White had left New York City for rural Maine and was writing about giving a pig an enema.

Nevertheless, White read and recommended George Santayana to improve one's sentence structure.[34] He read the poets of his acquaintance and sometimes poked fun there, too, as with "How to Tell a Major Poet From a Minor Poet."[35] He read *The New Yorker* writers—especially James Thurber, Joel Sayres, and John McNulty— to see what he was up against and keep his tone. He looked up to Robert Benchley, Frank Sullivan, and Ring Lardner, and knew the writers of the Algonquin Round Table (although he did not frequent it). Of his contemporaries, he was more apt to read H. L. Mencken or Christopher Morley than William Faulkner, Theodore Dreiser, or Willa Cather. Katharine was the avid reader, as a Bryn Mawr girl, then fiction editor and children's book reviewer, so stacks of books made their way through the household and their conversations, but not necessarily onto *his* reading list.

When Scott Elledge was working on White's biography, White wrote him an apologetic letter, saying:

> Congratulations on your manly attempt to make me into a literary character. It isn't going to work, but it makes great reading....It's an ironical twist of fate that my eyesight is failing just as I was about to sit down and read all the books I've never read. I had hoped to become literary just as I was crossing the finish line. But it's too late now. Can't see to do it. I did read Huckleberry Finn once, years ago, you will be relieved to know. And two years ago I began A. Karenina and finished it fourteen months later.[36]

He continued on the same track, two years later:

> One of the things that tickled me about the book was your obvious sadness at my not being a scholar or a poet, your disappointment that I was reading Don Marquis when I should have been reading Proust.[37]

Conversely, White continued to feel duty-bound to report items of natural and unnatural wonder, everything from the hatching of a goose egg to the failure of an American flag to "float on the breeze that does not blow" from the Moon.[38]

As White remarked on the occasion of receiving the National Medal for Literature, "As a writing man, or secretary, I have always felt charged with the safekeeping of all unexpected items of worldly and unworldly enchantment, as though I might be held personally responsible if even a small one were to be lost."[39] Perhaps because he was such a slow reader himself, White felt an obligation to be as clear and easily understood as possible. He did *not* feel an obligation to become a public figure, a speaker, a book reviewer, or blurb writer.

Our Hungry Critics

Andy White may have doubted his qualifications as a reader, but he wasn't afraid to ally himself with humorists, even while he acknowledged:

> The world likes humor, but it treats it patronizingly. It decorates its serious artists with laurel, and its wags with Brussels sprouts. It feels that if a thing is funny it can be presumed to be something less than great, because if it were truly great it would be wholly serious. Writers know this, and those who take their literary selves with great seriousness are at considerable pains never to associate their name with anything funny or flippant or nonsensical or "light." They suspect it would hurt their reputation, and they are right.[40]

Paul Gray, writing about White for *Time* magazine said, "Because he so consistently favored straight talk over polemics and specific details over abstractions, White has been dismissed in some quarters as a miniaturist a little too long on charm and short on substance."[41] In April, 1977, White noted the similarly disparaging attitude toward essayists:

> I tend still to fall back on the essay form (or lack of form) when an idea strikes me, but I am not fooled about the place of the essay in twentieth-century American letters—it stands a short distance down the line. The essayist, unlike the novelist, the poet, and the playwright, must be content in his self-imposed role of second-class citizen. A writer who has his sights trained on the Nobel Prize or other earthly triumphs had best write a novel, a poem, or a play, and leave the essayist to ramble about, content with living a free life and enjoying the satisfactions of a somewhat undisciplined existence.[42]

Other well-known essayists of the day—Mark Twain, James Baldwin, Richard Wright, F. Scott Fitzgerald, Eudora Welty, Vladimir Nabokov—were primarily known and rewarded for their novels, even though their occasional essays took on the big issues. White never attempted novels except those for children, and he was sometimes dismissed as *merely* a children's book writer, especially as sales of *Charlotte's Web* and *Stuart Little* crept into the millions.

In reality, White's primary work for nearly sixty years was as an essayist and his favorite essay form was the casual. In 1977, Herbert Mitgang called him "America's foremost essayist" and claimed that "White's essays have never stopped flourishing from season to season and book to book."[43] White took on the big issues of world government, freedom of speech, race, and the separation of church and state, but he did so in the form of short essays, and he tended to approach

24

his subjects by speaking about himself and what he had directly experienced. As he advised "young writers who want to get ahead without any annoying delays: don't write about Man, write about a man."[44]

White was apt to address the subject of security by speaking first about a Ferris wheel at the local county fair, or the subject of democracy from the perspective of roofing his barn and looking out across the bay. In part because he was so plainspoken, he was sometimes dismissed as not serious or not literary enough, just as a humorist risks being taken lightly because he makes light of a situation. The common thread in the books White admired (like *Walden*), or the politics he espoused, or the intellectual ideas he stood behind, however, was a solid anchor of integrity. He disparaged "moral fraudulence"[45] in the same way that Cornell's Professor Strunk had disparaged vague or irresolute writing; it was fuzzy thinking, and it would undermine the clarity of purpose and upright values that kept America strong. Words *always* made a difference.

Department of Straight Thinking

When White tackled the issue of civil liberties with the New York *Herald Tribune*, in 1947, for their support of blacklisting the "Hollywood Ten," people took note:

> I am a member of a party of one, and I live in an age of fear. Nothing lately has unsettled my party and raised my fears so much as your editorial, on Thanksgiving Day, suggesting that employees should be required to state their beliefs in order to hold their jobs. The idea is inconsistent with our Constitutional theory and has been stubbornly opposed by watchful men since the early days of the Republic. It's hard for me to believe that

E. B. White in the henhouse,
1939. White had increased
his flock during the war years.

the *Herald Tribune* is backing away from the fight, and I can only
assume that your editorial writer, in a hurry to get home for
Thanksgiving, tripped over the First Amendment and thought
it was the office cat.[46]

Justice Felix Frankfurter wrote to congratulate him on his ability to
"speak with the tongues of angels."[47] (The *Herald Tribune* continued
to disagree.) Years later, White stopped Xerox in its tracks with his
letter to the editor about Xerox's corporate sponsorships of *Esquire*
writers. *Esquire* was proposing to publish a travel article by Harrison

E. Salisbury, formerly of the *New York Times*, which would be paid for entirely by a Xerox Corporation sponsorship. White objected, "If magazines decide to farm out their writers to advertisers and accept the advertiser's payment to the writer and to the magazine, then the periodicals of this country will be far down the drain and will become so fuzzy as to be indistinguishable from the controlled press in other parts of the world."[48] White got a letter from W. B. Jones, the director of communications operations at Xerox, thanking him for "telling me what I didn't want to hear,"[49] and Xerox pulled the sponsorships.

One *New Yorker* obituary writer remembered it being said of White that he wrote as if neither Marx nor Freud had ever existed, "but he would not then set about becoming more political or more at one with his psyche. He never wished his readers to think him deeper or wiser than he found himself to be."[50] Even so, White's editorials on world government, nationalism, and loyalty in *The Wild Flag* showed he wasn't afraid to take on the weightier issues of the day. Harold Ross had used the formation of the United Nations to coax the Whites back to *The New Yorker*, and Andy must have felt duty-bound both to Ross and to the nation to take on political topics during the war years. Years later, White admitted that his essays had been idealistic, as some readers had argued at the time. Still, in 1961, White wrote that *The Wild Flag* "has grown whiskers...although I have no quarrel with its basic idea."[51]

Joseph Epstein, in his commentary "E. B. White, Dark & Lite,"[52] remembered Isaac Rosenfeld's "Chopping a Teakettle" review of *The Wild Flag*, its title taken from the Yiddish phrase *hackena tcheinik*. "Not only does he chop away with an unfailing stroke," Rosenfeld had written, "but he manages to keep a cloud of steam issuing from the spout as he works."[53] Epstein added, "The editorials in *The Wild Flag* are about world government, but before he lays down his ax, White has worked on several teakettles: the environment, bureaucracy, the horrors of modern life."[54]

27

Department of Elegance

By the late 1950s, White had moved firmly into the role of literary stylist. H. A. Stevenson, editor of the *Cornell Alumni News*, had sent him an early edition of William Strunk, Jr.'s writing manual, prompting White to write a fond reminiscence of his late professor. White's essay had ended, "Get the *little* book! Get the *little* book! Get the *little* book!"[55] This led Macmillan to suggest a reissue of the grammar book. White proposed revisions and an expanded Strunk & White's *The Elements of Style* was published in 1959. Since then, well over ten million copies have been sold. A new edition, illustrated by Maira Kalman, appeared in 2005.[56]

The style rules that White added to *The Elements of Style*—"Place yourself in the background; write in a way that comes naturally; do not affect a breezy manner";[57] and so forth—are pure White. Breezy manners were the stuff of spoof, to him. "The beginner should approach style warily, realizing it is himself he is approaching, no other."[58] In other words, be clear and be yourself. "Revise and rewrite," he advised, and he followed his own advice. I once witnessed him on hands and knees on the floor of his office in Maine, scissors in one hand, glue pot in the other, cutting a manuscript apart, and pasting it together again, long before the days of word processors. Cornell now houses over one hundred linear feet of his shelved letters and papers, much of it the revisions that survived these cut and paste sessions.

In 1994, Peter F. Neumeyer published *The Annotated Charlotte's Web* in an attempt to explain how White did what he did. Neumeyer wrote, "White's sense of style was demanding; one jots in his margins with trepidation."[59]

Dissecting style is not unlike dissecting humor, or music, or any other artistic expression, however. One can study early drafts and revisions and final versions and still not know why an author chose one word and discarded another. Clear thinking and a good ear enhance the process, but ultimately style is as individual as the writer.

James Thurber, John Updike, Andy Rooney, Charles Kuralt, and countless others have spoken of White as an early mentor and guide. Generations of students and professionals have kept *The Elements of Style* at their fingertips, long after they graduated from English 101. Modern novelists who believe in heavy revisions often mention White. As an example, John Irving—who quotes E. B. White repeatedly in his 2001 novel *The Fourth Hand*—has remarked that rewriting is what he does *best*, as a writer, that he spends more time on it than on the initial draft. In that, at least, he has emulated White. One of Irving's fictional characters, Dr. Zajac, even attempts to revise his relationship with his son by reading E. B. White's children's books to him, and oddly it seems to work—perhaps one for White's *Raised Eyebrows Department.*

Up Life's Ladder

At mid-century, colleges and universities began to bestow honorary degrees on White, starting with Dartmouth, the University of Maine, and Yale (all in 1948, perhaps because of his efforts for world peace) and followed in the 1950s by Bowdoin, Hamilton, Harvard, and Colby.

In 1927, when Charles Lindbergh flew his non-stop flight from New York to Paris, White penned a "Notes and Comment" piece that began, "We noted that the Spirit of St. Louis had not left the ground ten minutes before it was joined by the Spirit of Me Too."[60] Likewise, a couple of years later, he wrote:

> This, by the way, is the time of year we get fairly bitter about the honorary (uh huh) degrees that universities confer on illustrious

E. B. White (back row, center) receiving an honorary degree from
Yale in 1948. Note that General Dwight D. Eisenhower was also
receiving an honorary degree that year (front row, 2nd from
left). Courtesy of the Division of Rare and Manuscript
Collections, Cornell University Library.

citizens. Not all universities are guilty of this prestige-swapping
ritual, but most of them are.... When we observe a university
handing out honorary degrees, we suspect it of about the same
motives as those of Arthur Schreiber, the aerial stowaway; we
suspect it of wanting to get in on something.[61]

In 1953, White received a Newbery honor for *Charlotte's Web,* followed
by a Gold Medal for Essays and Criticism from the National Institute
of Arts and Letters, in 1960.

After White's death in 1985, an editorial cartoon circulated widely, depicting a sad Wilbur under Charlotte's web that contained the words: SOME WRITER.[62] Joseph Epstein's *Time* essay mentioned it, with his comment, "Some career." Epstein said White may have been "the most honored American writer of our time. He had more medals than a Soviet marshal" including "a special—and, so far as I know, unique—Pulitzer Prize for 'the body of his work.' "[63]

News of an earlier award, the prestigious Presidential Medal of Freedom had arrived on July 1, 1963, in the form of a telegram. White wrote to Cushman, his old travel companion, to describe President John F. Kennedy's long-winded telephone wire about the recipients, chosen for "meritorious contribution to the security or national interests of the United States, world peace, cultural or other significant public or private endeavor" and how Katharine had "dutifully scribbled the first thirty or forty words on a scratch pad," then asked the Western Union girl on the phone, "Is this a practical joke?"[64]

Sadly, just four months later, White was writing President Kennedy's obituary for *The New Yorker*.[65] The Presidential medals were awarded in December by Kennedy's successor, Lyndon Baines Johnson. White did not attend, but he was pleased to have Maine's then Senator Edmund Muskie hang it around his neck the following year.

More prizes and medals followed and ultimately White was named a Pulitzer Prize winner, given a Special Award and Citation (1978) "for his letters, essays and the full body of his work." He wrote to Muskie, a U.S. senator by then, recalling the earlier occasion and remarking: "Thanks for your congratulatory note on my Pulitzer citation. Even at my age, I'd be glad to swap off with you and be asked to crown a beauty queen."[66] He might have done so, if it hadn't meant a public appearance; he could write a speech, but he was loathe to deliver one.

White regretted that Katharine had missed the big one, which would have meant more to her than to him; she had died of congestive heart failure in 1977. He wrote a friend, saying Kay "would have been pleased with my Pulitzer award, and life without her is no bargain for me, awards or no awards. She was the one great award in my life and I am in awe of having received it."[67] As in the early days at *The New Yorker*, White's seeming disregard of social expectations only increased with age and fame. He didn't speak, wasn't a member of clubs or associations, rarely granted interviews, turned down editorships, and even said no to the Book-of-the-Month Club. James Russell Wiggins, formerly of the *Washington Post* and, later, editor of Maine's weekly the *Ellsworth American*, recalled White as "a master non-attender."[68] He almost never appeared on stage, because he felt physically incapable of the task, the result of what he called his "natural uneasiness and fear of platforms."[69] At White's funeral, his stepson Roger Angell remembered White's avoidance of ceremonial occasions, saying, "If [he] could have been here today, he wouldn't have been here."[70]

After White's biographer, Scott Elledge, spent sixteen years researching *E. B. White: A Biography*, the jacket flap billed White as "America's most beloved writer."[71] That made White squirm when he saw it on the proofs, and he wrote a letter to an old friend, saying, "I have already told Scott what a mistake that is, since people really want to read about someone they can loathe."[72]

Speaking as a former advertising man, White warned Elledge that the phrase "isn't a good pulling idea."[73] To his friend, he added, "After all, I'm no Norman Mailer, with his seven wives and occasional knifings. Nobody in his right mind would pick me for the subject of a biography."[74] After reading the galleys, White offered Elledge an alternative jacket blurb: "Quite simply, the best in-depth study ever, made of an out-of-his-depth man. Hilarious."[75]

As early as the 1960s, White was beginning to assemble his papers for the Division of Rare and Manuscript Collections at the Cornell

University Library, delighted that they would lighten his decades-long accumulation of letters and manuscripts. In 1976, he had published his first book of letters, compiled with the help of his wife Katharine and his goddaughter, Dorothy Lobrano Guth. The resulting mail from its publication, and then from Katharine's death the following year, was overwhelming.

A *New York Times* obituary by Herbert Mitgang called White "one of the nation's most precious literary resources," his children's books "classics" and his importance to students "immeasurable."[76] The *Times* gave him a six-column-across spread, which Joseph Epstein likened to "the kind it generally grants only to indisputably major statesmen and artists."[77] *The New Yorker*'s editor, William Shawn, said:

> E. B. White was a great essayist, a supreme stylist. His literary style was as pure as any in our language. It was singular, colloquial, clear, unforced, thoroughly American and utterly beautiful. Because of his quiet influence, several generations of this country's writers write better than they might have done. He never wrote a mean or careless sentence. He was impervious to literary, intellectual and political fashion. He was ageless, and his writing was timeless.[78]

In 1999, on the one-hundredth anniversary of White's birth, his well-known "Here Is New York" essay (1949) was reprinted in book form, because of the beauty and grace of its prose. Earlier, Edwin M. Yoder, Jr., in a *Washington Post* obituary, had claimed White "was one of those writer's writers who shaped the modern American idiom. His music will haunt us all for a long time."[79] After the September 11, 2001 tragedy, White's haunting and musical "Here Is New York" essay took on new meaning, not only for the beauty of the prose but because of its timeless forewarning:

> A single flight of planes no bigger than a wedge of geese can quickly end this island fantasy, burn the towers, crumble the bridges, turn the underground passages into lethal chambers, cremate the millions. The intimation of mortality is part of New York now: in the sound of jets overhead, in the black headlines of the latest edition.[80]

Benjamin DeMott, reviewing *Essays of E. B. White*, also spoke of the *sound* of his words: "What is beyond criticism in a White essay is the music. The man knows all the tunes, all the limited lovely music that a plain English sentence can play."[81] Here was a man who could not only tell us what we didn't want to know, but tell us beautifully.

Yoder saw White as "a very serious writer indeed," but one who used a "toned-down, scaled-down, minimalist language, [in which] democracy isn't a fixed system of beliefs, it is a 'recurrent suspicion... a song that hasn't gone bad.'"[82] Yoder noted only one "eminent rival" to White in this deflationary tone: Ernest Hemingway. "Eventually, this voice of urbane deflation will be seen as a 20th century American landmark," Yoder argued, "as eloquent in what it says about 20th century American civilization as the Empire State Building or the space shuttle. Social historians will have the interesting task of explaining why the two most distinctive voices in American prose so similarly recoiled from abstraction and elocution."[83]

Sentences We Hated to Come to the End Of

Years earlier, White had written to his brother, Stanley: "I can remember, really quite distinctly, looking a sheet of paper square in the eyes when I was seven or eight years old and thinking 'This is where I belong, this is it.' "[84] When White was named to the National Institute of Arts and Letters, Stan had sent a congratulatory gift of "white bond, with rag content," and White assured him that "at this late day, a blank sheet of paper holds the greatest excitement there is for me—more promising than a silver cloud, prettier than a little red wagon. It holds all the hope there is, all fears."[85] Nearly four decades later, at the end of White's life, those hopes and fears had diminished but slightly, and his remarkable sense of wonder remained strong.

Critics had been calling his works classics even before he died. William Shawn, editor of *The New Yorker* when White died in 1985, credited him with having "developed a new literary form" in his paragraphs for the magazine. Shawn said that White "left his mark on every page of the magazine, and his presence continues, and will always continue, to be felt in our pages. Ross was so enchanted with White's work that he had moments when he wished that all writers were E. B. White."[86] Thankfully, all writers are *not* E. B. White, despite Ross's fond wishes. As a grandfather, as a writer, and as a stylist, White was one of a kind.

Roger Angell recalled Joel reading to his father during Andy's last year, after White had been diagnosed with senile dementia. Although he continued to recognize family and friends, his mind drifted to happier times. Books remained a pleasure, however, so my father would stop by on his way home from work. In his memoir, *Let Me Finish*, Angell wrote:

> [Joel] would read aloud to his father and discovered that he enjoyed listening to his own writings, though he wasn't always clear about who the author was. Sometimes he'd raise a hand and impatiently wave a passage away: not good enough. Other evenings he'd listen until the end…and then ask again who'd

E. B. White rowing out to his sloop, *Martha*, with his son's Brooklin Boat Yard in the background, October 1976. Photo courtesy of Kathy Romans Hall, editor for *E. B. White, A Bibliographic Catalogue.*

written these words. "You did, Dad," Joe said. There was a pause and Andy said, "Well, not bad."[87]

In 1940, White had written an essay called "Maine Speech," explaining local words like "baster" (pronounced bayster) or "spleeny" (sensitive to cold) or "dozy" (unseasoned wood).[88] In many ways, things in Maine are not so different today. My older brother (the ol' baster) runs the boatyard that our father founded, and my younger brother (the avid ping-pong player) continues to fish out of the small town where we grew up, though he's spleenier than he used to be. Ask any lobsterman how he's doing, even in the most bountiful years when the legal-sized lobsters or "keepers" are plentiful, and he's apt to say, in classic understatement, "Not bad." So, for that "simple and sincere account" of E. B. White's place in twentieth century literary history, I echo White's self-critique of the best of his own works, high praise indeed: "Well, not bad." Or, as we'd say here in Maine, he's a keeper.

Martha White

Rockport, Maine

Notes

1. "The Sea and the Wind That Blows," 1963; *Essays of E. B. White* (New York: Harper & Row, 1977). p. 207.

2. Letter to Martha White, December 8, 1971; *Letters of E. B. White*, Rev. Ed. (New York: HarperCollins, 2006), p. 579–580.

3. E. B. White unpublished journal entry, "Thursday, November 26, [1964], Thanksgiving Day, 9:15 p.m.," Collection of the White Literary LLC.

4. "Questionnaire," May, 1942; *One Man's Meat* (New York, Harper & Row, 1942), p. 234.

5. "The Ring of Time," March 22, 1956; *Essays of E. B. White*, p. 142.

6. "What Do Our Hearts Treasure?" January, 1966; Ibid., p. 150.

7. Ibid., p. 153.

8. "Mount Vernon, 1908–1917," *Letters of E. B. White*, Rev. Ed., p. 6.

9. Letter to Albert White, October 21, 1908; *E. B. White: A Biography*, by Scott Elledge (New York: W.W. Norton, 1984), p. 30.

10. "Notes and Comment," April 2, 1960; *The New Yorker*, p. 31.

11. "The Years of Wonder," March 13, 1961; *Essays of E. B. White*, p. 169.

12. "The Bowling Green," November, 1923, *New York Evening Post*; and *E. B. White: A Biography*, p. 98.

13. "A Step Forward," April 18, 1925; *The New Yorker*, p. 21.

14. "Defense of the Bronx River," May 9, 1925; *The New Yorker*, p. 14.

15. "The New Yorker—Early Days, 1926–1928," *Letters of E. B. White*, Rev. Ed., p. 70.

16. Letter to Stanley Hart White, January 1929; Ibid., p. 82.

17. Cover art by E. B. White, *The New Yorker*, April 23, 1932.

18. Letter to Katharine S. White, May 31, 1937; *Letters of E. B. White*, Rev. Ed., p. 145.

19. "Introduction," May, 1982; *One Man's Meat*, p. xiii.

20. Letter from Jean Stafford to E. B. White, Fall, 1952; in *E. B. White: A Biography*, p. 298.

21. "Life in the Barn Was Very Good," by Eudora Welty, October 19, 1952; *Sunday New York Times Book Review*.

22. Dale E. Haskell, "The Rhetoric of the Familiar Essay: E. B. White and Personal Discourse" (PhD diss., Texas Christian University, 1983).

23. Diana Trilling review of *One Man's Meat*, August 8, 1942; *Nation*.

24. William Soskin, October 10, 1934; *New York American*, quoted in *E. B. White: A Biography*, pp. 190–191.

25. "What Am I Saying to My Readers?" May 14, 1961; Book section, *New York Times*.

26. "Visitors to the Pond," May 23, 1953; *The New Yorker*, p. 28.

27. "Talk of the Town," August 7, 1948; *The New Yorker*, p. 13.

28. "A Slight Sound at Evening," Summer, 1954; *Essays of E. B. White*, p. 237.

29. "Visitors to the Pond," p. 28.

30. "A Slight Sound at Evening," p. 235.

31. "E. B. W." by James Thurber, *Saturday Review of Literature*, October 15, 1938.

32. *Here Is New York* (1949; New York: Little Bookroom, 1999), pp. 37–38.

33. "Across the Street and Into the Grill," October 14, 1950; *Second Tree from the Corner* (New York: Harper & Bros., 1954), p. 140.

34. Letter to Katharine S. White, April 27, 1938; and letter to Faith McNulty Martin, March 11, [1963?]; *Letters of E. B. White*, Rev. Ed., pp. 165, 450.

35. "How to Tell a Major Poet from a Minor Poet," November 8, 1930; *The New Yorker*, pp. 23–24.

36. Letter to Scott Elledge, May, 25, 1982; *Letters of E.B. White*, Rev. Ed., p. 648.

37. Letter to Scott Elledge, February 10, 1984; Ibid., pp. 676–677.

38. "Moon Landing," July 26, 1969; *E. B. White: Writings from* The New Yorker, *1925–1976*; Rebecca M. Dale, ed. (New York: HarperCollins, 1990), p. 102.

39. "The Egg Is All," December 7, 1971; remarks on receiving the National Medal for Literature, Book section, *New York Times*.

40. "Some Remarks on Humor," 1941; *Essays of E. B. White*, p. 244.

41. "A Master of Luminous Prose," by Paul Gray, October 14, 1985; *Time*, p. 105.

42. "Foreword," April, 1977; *Essays of E. B. White*, p. vii.

43. "Behind the Best Sellers," by Herbert Mitgang, November 20, 1977; *New York Times*.

44. "Some Remarks on Humor," p. 246.

45. *E. B. White: A Biography*, p. 209.

46. Letter to the *New York Herald Tribune*, November 29, 1947; *Letters of E. B. White*, Rev. Ed., p. 267.

47. Footnote to a letter to Felix Frankfurter, December 12, 1947; Ibid., p. 269.

48. Letter to the editor of the *Ellsworth American*, January 1, 1976; Ibid., p. 612.

49. Footnote to a letter to W. B. Jones, January 30, 1976; Ibid., p. 615.

50. "Notes and Comment," E. B. White obituary comments by William Shawn, John Updike, and Roger Angell, October 14, 1985; *New Yorker*, pp. 31–33.

51. Letter to Paul Brooks, December 13, 1961; *Letters of E. B. White*, Rev. Ed., p. 445.

52. "E.B. White, Dark & Lite," by Joseph Epstein, April, 1986; *Commentary Magazine*.

53. "Chopping a Teakettle," by Isaac Rosenfeld, December 28, 1946; *Nation*.

54. "E.B. White, Dark & Lite."

55. "Will Strunk," July 15, 1957; *Essays of E. B. White*, p. 261.

56. *The Elements of Style*, by Strunk & White, illustrated by Maira Kalman (New York: Penguin Press, 2005).

57. "An Approach to Style," in *The Elements of Style*, by Strunk and White, pp. 59–78.

58. Ibid., p. 62.

59. Peter F. Neumeyer, *The Annotated Charlotte's Web* (New York: HarperCollins, 1994), p. xviii.

60. "Notes and Comment," May 28, 1927; *The New Yorker*, p. 11.

61. "Notes and Comment," June 29, 1929; *The New Yorker*, p. 9.

62. "SOME WRITER," Obituary Cartoon, October, 1985; *(Caption: E. B. White: 1899–1985) Des Moines Register*, by Brian Duffy.

63. "E.B. White, Dark & Lite."

64. Letter to Howard Cushman, July 9 [1963]; *Letters of E. B. White*, Rev. Ed., p. 456.

65. "John F. Kennedy," November 30, 1963; *E. B. White: Writings from The New Yorker*, p. 102.

66. Letter to The Hon. Edmund S. Muskie [May 1, 1978]; *Letters of E. B. White*, Rev. Ed., p. 621.

67. Letter to Gluyas Williams [May 8, 1978]; Ibid., p. 621.

68. Eulogy for E. B. White by Russell Wiggins of the *Ellsworth American*, October 26, 1985; Blue Hill Congregational Church, Blue Hill, Maine.

69. *E. B. White: A Biography*, p. 22.

70. Remarks by Roger Angell, in memory of his stepfather, E. B. White, October 26, 1985; Blue Hill Congregational Church, Blue Hill, Maine.

71. *E. B. White: A Biography*, inside jacket flap.

72. Letter to Mrs. Susan [Lovenburg] Robinson, [January 1984]; *Letters of E. B. White*, Rev. Ed., p. 672.

73. Letter to Ann Honeycutt [June 12, 1983]; Ibid., p. 665.

74. Ibid.

75. Letter to Scott Elledge [May 28, 1983]; Ibid., p. 665.

76. "E.B. White, Essayist and Stylist, Dies," by Herbert Mitgang, October 2, 1985; *New York Times*, p. B9.

77. "E.B. White, Dark & Lite."

78. William Shawn quoted in "E. B. White, Essayist and Stylist, Dies," by Herbert Mitgang, October 2, 1985; *New York Times*.

79. "E. B. White: Urbane, Understated and an American Treasure," by Edwin M. Yoder, Jr., Washington Post Writers Group, October 1985.

80. *Here Is New York*, p. 54.

81. Benjamin Demott, review of *Essays of E. B. White* in *Saturday Review*, August 20, 1977, p. 63.

82. "E. B. White: Urbane, Understated and an American Treasure."

83. Ibid.

84. Letter to Stanley White [January, 1947]; *Letters of E. B. White*, Rev. Ed., pp. 263–264.

85. Ibid.

86. "Notes and Comment," E. B. White obituary comments by William Shawn, p. 31.

87. Roger Angell, *Let Me Finish* (New York: Harcourt, 2006), p. 137.

88. "Maine Speech," October, 1940; *One Man's Meat*, p. 154.

E. B. WHITE CHRONOLOGY

1899, July 11
Elwyn Brooks White was born to Samuel Tilly White and Jessie (Hart) White in Mount Vernon, New York, the youngest of six children: Marion, Clara, Albert, Stanley, Lillian, and Elwyn.

1913–1917
Attended Mount Vernon High School; published in the school's *Oracle*.

1917–1921
Enrolled at Cornell University; earned his nickname, Andy, after Cornell's first president, Andrew D. White.

1918
Registered for the draft, but was rejected for not weighing enough. Enlisted in the Student Army Training Corps at Cornell. (Armistice was declared in November.)

1920
Editor-in-Chief at the *Cornell Daily Sun*.

1921

Graduated from Cornell. Declined a teaching position and went to work (briefly) for the United Press and later the American Legion News Service.

1922

Cross-country road trip with Cornell classmate, Howard Cushman, in White's Model T Ford, Hotspur. Work along the way included the publication of a sonnet to a Kentucky Derby horse, winning a limerick contest, selling roach powder, playing the piano, and hocking their typewriters. Took a job with the *Seattle Times*.

1923

Left for Alaska on the *S.S. Buford;* worked on the ship to earn his return passage. Returned to New York City and took various unsatisfying jobs in advertising, while submitting pieces to "The Conning Tower" and other publications.

1925, February 19

The New Yorker's first issue; White published in the April 18, 1925 issue ("A Step Forward; The Advertising Man Takes Over the Vernal Account," and next in the May 9, 1925 issue: "Defense of the Bronx River," and others.

1926

Began part-time work for *The New Yorker*.

1927

Accepted a full-time position at *The New Yorker*.

1929

The Lady Is Cold; Is Sex Necessary? (co-authored with James Thurber); married Katharine (Sergeant) Angell, November 13.

1930

Son Joel McCoun White born, December 21.

1931

Published *Ho-Hum: Newsbreaks from* The New Yorker, with illustrations by O. Soglow.

1932

Published *Another Ho-Hum;* April 23 contributed a *New Yorker* cover, a watercolor painting of a seahorse with an oat bag.

1933

Purchased salt water farm in Brooklin, Maine on Allen Cove.

1934

Published *Every Day Is Saturday.*

1935

Death of White's father, Samuel Tilley White.

1936

Published *Farewell to Model T* (with Richard Lee Strout, published under the name Lee Strout White); death of White's mother, Jessie Hart White.

1937

White's "Year of Grace" from *The New Yorker,* "Talk of the Town" farewell on August 7, 1937, and subsequent move to Maine.

1938

Published *The Fox of Peapack and Other Poems;* began "One Man's Meat" column for *Harper's* magazine.

1939

Published *Quo Vadimus?*

1941

Published *A Subtreasury of American Humor*, edited, with K. S. White.

1942

Published *One Man's Meat.*

1945

Published *Stuart Little.*

1946

Published *The Wild Flag.*

1948

Awarded honorary degrees from Dartmouth, University of Maine, and Yale.

1949

Published *Here Is New York.*

1950

Awarded an honorary degree from Bowdoin College.

1952

Published *Charlotte's Web;* received Hamilton honorary degree.

1953

Received Newbery honor for *Charlotte's Web.*

1954

Published *The Second Tree from the Corner;* received honorary degrees from Harvard University and Colby College.

1959

Published *The Elements of Style* (Strunk and White).

1960

Received Gold Medal for Essays and Criticism from the National Institute of Arts and Letters.

1962

Published *The Points of My Compass.*

1963

Received Presidential Medal of Freedom, from President John F. Kennedy (presented by Maine's Senator Edmund Muskie, in 1964)

1970

Published *Trumpet of the Swan;* received Laura Ingalls Wilder Medal.

1971

Received National Medal for Literature.

1973

Elected to the American Academy of Arts and Letters.

1976

The Letters of E. B. White, edited by Dorothy Lobrano Guth, is published

1977

Essays of E. B. White is published; death of Katharine Sergeant White, after nearly forty-eight years of marriage.

1978

Received Pulitzer Prize special citation for letters.

1979

Onward and Upward in the Garden, by Katharine S. White, is published (Edited and with an Introduction by E. B. White).

1981

Published *Poems and Sketches of E. B. White.*

1984

E. B. White: A Biography, by Scott Elledge, is published.

1985, October I—

Death of E. B. White, at his home in North Brooklin, Maine.

1990

Writings from The New Yorker, *1925–1976,* edited by Rebecca M. Dale, is published.

1996

White on White, audio recording of E. B. White selections, read by Joel White, appeared.

2006

The Letters of E. B. White (Revised Edition), edited by Martha White, is published.

THE WORDS OF E. B. WHITE

Aging
(see also Childhood, Youth)

Beginnings
I was born in 1899, which was a big mistake. Should have waited.
—Letter to Eleanor Gould Packard, October 20, 1982; The E. B.
White Collection, Carl A. Kroch Library, Cornell University,
Ithaca, NY.

You know what they were doing, don't you, the year I was born—
they were beginning to demolish the reservoir at 42nd and Fifth to
make way for a public library to house the books that little Elwyn
White would write when he got big enough to hold a pencil. I saw my
first circus in Stanford White's yellow brick Madison Square Garden,
holding tight my father's hand. I covered the opening of the Roxy and
the Paramount for *Talk*....
—Letter to Carol and Roger Angell,* January 9, 1967; *Letters of
E. B. White*, Rev. Ed., p. 497.
   * For Christmas, White had been given *Lost New York*, by Nathan
   Silver.

Children are radicals. Youths are conservatives, with a dash of criminal negligence. Men in their prime are liberals (as long as their digestion keeps pace with their intellect).

    —"Life Phases," February 20, 1937; *Writings from* The New Yorker, *1925–1976,* p. 112.

His woes, through being often stated,
Have grown, of late, attenuated,
And so he stirs the cosmic rubble
And writes of other people's trouble,
Astonishingly fit to shoulder
The heaviest sort of human boulder,
They say that he has gone a year
And not let fall one honest tear—

Except a very tiny one
Upon a line he wrote in fun.

    — "POET, Or the Growth of a Lit'ry Figure" (excerpt), April 6, 1929; *The New Yorker.*

Middle Age

The middle-aged, except in rare cases, run to shelter: they insure their life, draft a will, accumulate mementos and occasional tables, and hope for security. And then comes old age, which repeats childhood—a time full of humors and sadness, but often full of courage and even prophecy.

    —"Life Phases," February 20, 1937; *Writings from* The New Yorker, *1925–1976,* p. 112.

I was thirty-eight years old today, and spent most of the day trying to build a henyard—which seems an odd milestone. The planks seemed heavy, and I noticed that I quit early and took a drink.

    —Letter to Charles G. Muller, July 11, 1937; *Letters of E. B. White,* Rev. Ed., p. 149.

It is in his fifty-to-seventy phase that a man pulls in his ears, lashes down his principles, and gets ready for dirty weather.

    —"Life Phases," February 20, 1937; *Writings from* The New Yorker, *1925–1976,* p. 112.

Before he reached the age of ten
The poet lived like other men.
Before he reached the age of twenty
He fell in love and suffered plenty.
And when he lyrically hinted
That life was tragic, it was printed.

The song he played upon his pipe
Looked rather well, he thought, in type.

    —"POET, Or the Growth of a Lit'ry Figure" (excerpt), April 6, 1929; *The New Yorker.*

Old Age

At seventy, men are just beginning to grow liberal again, after a decade or two of conservatism.

    —"Life Phases," February 20, 1937; *Writings from* The New Yorker, *1925–1976,* p. 111.

The men of eighty whom we know are on the whole a more radical, rip-snorting lot than the men of seventy. They hold life cheaply, and hence are able to entertain generous thoughts about the state.

—"Life Phases," February 20, 1937; *Writings from* The New Yorker, *1925–1976*, pp. 111–112.

Octogenarians have a more devil-may-care tactic: they are sometimes quite willing to crowd on some sail and see if they can't get a burst of speed out of the old hooker yet.

—"Life Phases," February 20, 1937; *Writings from* The New Yorker, *1925–1976*, p. 112.

Today I read an entry in my journal—about 1924 or 1925—telling of an evening at 48 Mersereau, when Father and I played a game of poker after supper and Mother sat alone playing Parcheesi against an imaginary opponent, whose moves she made. The loneliness of old age struck me and I set it down on paper—a young man observing his parents. And now I know of it, not as an observer but at first hand. Every time I go back into my journals I am shaken by them—by how tantalizing they are, how awful they are, how little they tell (of events, places, people) and how much they reveal.

—Unpublished journal entry, June 20, 1965, 10:25 p.m.; White Literary LLC archive.

Israel Shenker's visit to this decadent ranch a couple weeks ago was not one of those perfect occasions that we all dream about.* I greeted him with tachycardia and taciturnity in about equal parts, and I guess he left without a story, because I soon received an abominable questionnaire in the mail and had no choice but to sit down and answer it. Between the two of us, the Times's celebration of my 70th acquired the taste of stale fruit-cake and reminded me of Morris Bishop's

remark some years ago when he read an interview with me by a Cornell co-ed: "You sounded like Ecclesiastes."
  —Letter to Frank Sullivan, July 14, 1969; *Letters of E. B. White*, Rev. Ed., p. 528.
    * Israel Shenker had come to North Brooklin, Maine to interview White for the *New York Times* on the occasion of his seventieth birthday.

Old age is a special problem for me because I've never been able to shed the mental image I have of myself—a lad of about nineteen.
  —"E. B. White: Notes and Comment by Author," interview with Israel Shenker, July 11, 1969*; *New York Times* and reprinted by Borealis Press on a greeting card.
    * July 11, 1969, was White's seventieth birthday.

How should one adjust to age? In principle, one shouldn't adjust. In fact, one does. (Or I do.) When my head starts knocking because of my attempt to write, I quit writing instead of carrying on as I used to do when I was young. These are adjustments. But I gaze into the faces of our senior citizens in our Southern cities, and they wear a sad look that disturbs me. I am sorry for all those who have agreed to grow old. I haven't agreed yet.
  —"E. B. White: Notes and Comment by Author," interview with Israel Shenker, July 11, 1969; *New York Times.*

A writer certainly has a special problem with aging. The generative process is slowed down, yet the pain and frustration of not writing is as acute as ever. I feel frustrated and in pain a good deal of the time now; but I try to bear in mind the advice of Hubert Humphrey's father. "Never get sick, Hubert; there isn't time."
  —"E. B. White: Notes and Comment by Author," interview with Israel Shenker, July 11, 1969; *New York Times.*

As for writing, I still write—at age 72. My experience is that I have to struggle harder, tire sooner, and come apart at the seams more completely than was the case when I was young.

— Letter to Maurice Root, November 15, 1971; *Letters of E. B. White*, Rev. Ed., p. 578.

I do not recall that he [Robert Benchley] ever "announced his retirement" from writing. There's no such thing as retiring from writing. You just run out of gas.

— Letter to Gerald Nachman, March 15, 1980; *Letters of E. B. White*, Rev. Ed., p. 632.

Thanks for "Happy to be Here" and for the inscription. I am happy to have this book. I haven't read it yet—at 82 there is no time for reading. The morning is taken up with lacing the shoes and buttoning the shirt, working with arthritic fingers solemnly and doggedly. The afternoon is spent sleeping, recovering from the luncheon drink. I can't remember how the evening is spent, but it is not spent reading— because of the slow progressive macula degeneration of the retina.

— Letter to Garrison Keillor, January?, 1981; *Letters of E. B. White*, Rev. Ed., p. 637.

I used to eat rhubarb because I loved rhubarb. Now I eat it because it retards arthritis.

— "Introduction," May, 1982; *One Man's Meat*, p. xiii.

How am I? Well, I'm 84, which doesn't help any. I have a first degree heart block and a 15-foot green Old Town canoe. First one wins, then the other.

— Letter to Pennell Peck, ca. August 20,1983; *Letters of E. B. White*, Rev. Ed., p. 668.

Last week I fell asleep while eating lunch alone at the dining table and crashed to the floor. After seven years of eating lunch alone, I apparently find sleep more attractive than food. A normal man of 84 would have broken a hip, but I didn't break anything, except another lousy record.

 —Letter to Mrs. Dorothy Guth, ca. March 16, 1984; *Letters of E. B. White*, Rev. Ed., pp. 678–679.

Welcome to the club!

As one who turned eighty-five in July, I have a message for you: Don't fall down. I waited what I thought was a decent interval, then fell on rough ground and broke a couple of ribs. There is no way to get to sleep when your ribs are broken, so you stay awake, turning things over in your mind—what's left of it.

I hope you have a nice party, and I hope you live as many more years as you can be either useful or happy or both. Stay on your feet, it's the place to be!

 —Letter to John R. Fleming, September 12, 1984; *Letters of E. B. White*, Rev. Ed., p. 684.

Airplanes

The curse of flight is speed. Or, rather, the curse of flight is that no opportunity exists for dawdling.

 —"Heavier Than Air," *Second Tree from the Corner*, p. 119, and *Notes on Our Times*, p. 63.

As for the skies, I quit using the flying machines in 1929 after the pilot of one of them, blinded by snow, handed the chart to me and asked *me* to find the Cleveland airport.

—"The Egg Is All," *New York Times*, December 7, 1971; remarks on receiving the National Medal for Literature.

Animals
(see Birds, Chickens, Cows, Dogs, Rats)

Atomic Age
(see also Doom, Nationalism, Peace)

Nuclear energy and foreign policy cannot coexist on the planet. The more deep the secret, the greater the determination of every nation to discover and exploit it. Nuclear energy insists on global government, on law, on order, and on the willingness of the community to take the responsibility for the acts of the individual.

—*The Wild Flag*, August 18, 1945, p. 109.

The only condition more appalling, less practical, than world government is the lack of it in this atomic age. Most of the scientists who produced the bomb admit that. Nationalism and the split atom cannot coexist in the planet.

—*The Wild Flag*, June 1, 1946, p. 186.

I've had a number of requests to reprint "The Morning of the Day They Did It," and have said no to them all.

Got my reasons. One reasons is that I'm not sure it's a public service to describe the end of the world, even in a spirit of satire. People are jumpy, right now, and I see no reason to explode paper bags.

—Letter to Earle Davis, October 27, 1950; *Letters of E. B. White*, Rev. Ed., p. 299.

The terror of the atom age is not the violence of the new power but the speed of man's adjustment to it—the speed of his acceptance.

—"The Age of Dust," *Second Tree from the Corner*, 1954, p. 115, and *Notes on Our Times*, p. 48.

Our complaint about the crisis is not that it is so appalling but that it is so trivial. The consequences of the atomic cataclysm that are being relentlessly published seem mild alongside the burning loveliness of a fall morning, or the flash of a south-bound bird, or the wry smell of chrysanthemums in the air.... The light of day—so hard at times to see, so convincing when seen.

—"Daylight and Darkness," *Second Tree from the Corner*, 1954, p. 128, and *Notes on Our Times*, p. 98.

[Man] knows that the atomic age is capable of delivering a new package of energy; what he doesn't know is whether it will prove to be a blessing.

—"The Distant Music of the Hounds," *Second Tree from the Corner*, 1954, p. 133, and *Notes on Our Times*, p. 112.

I am not convinced that atomic energy, which is currently said to be man's best hope for a better life, is his best hope at all, or even a good bet. I am not sure energy is his basic problem, although the weight of opinion is against me.

—"Coon Tree," June 14, 1956; *Points of My Compass*, p. 67, and *Essays of E. B. White*, p. 39.

A nation wearing atomic armor is like a knight whose armor has grown so heavy he is immobilized; he can hardly walk, hardly sit his horse, hardly think, hardly breathe.

—"Sootfall and Fallout," October 18, 1956; *Points of My Compass*, p. 82, and *Essays of E. B. White*, p. 94.

Automobiles

Everything in life is somewhere else, and you get there in a car.
—"Fro-Joy," January, 1940; *One Man's Meat,* p. 109.

Our idea for improving the taxicab situation is to change the design of the cabs. There should be, first, an emergency exit, through which passengers can escape unnoticed when the driving gets too awful. Second, there should be a doctor in each cab. Above all, there should be a signal board in front of the driver, operated from the back seat. This board would flash typical instructions, epithetical and threatening.
— "Notes and Comment," June 29, 1929; *The New Yorker.*

During my association with Model T's, self-starters were not a prevalent accessory. They were expensive and under suspicion. Your car came equipped with a serviceable crank, and the first thing you learned was how to Get Results.... The trick was to leave the ignition switch off, proceed to the animal's head, pull the choke... and give the crank two or three nonchalant upward lifts. Then, whistling as though thinking about something else, you would saunter back to the driver's cabin, turn the ignition on, return to the crank, and this time, catching it on the down stroke, give it a quick spin with plenty of that. If this procedure was followed, the engine almost always responded—first with a few scattered explosions, then with a tumultuous gunfire, which you checked by racing around to the driver's seat and retarding the throttle. Often, if the emergency brake hadn't been pulled all the way back, the car advanced on you the instant the first explosion occurred and you would hold it back by leaning your weight against it. I can still feel my

THE WORDS OF E. B. WHITE

old Ford nuzzling me at the curb, as though looking for an apple in my pocket.

—"Farewell, My Lovely!" ca. 1936,* *Essays of E. B. White,* p. 165, and *Farewell to Model T; From Sea to Shining Sea,* pp. 16–17.

* An excerpt of this much-reprinted essay was run in "Takes" in the seventy-fifth anniversary issue of *The New Yorker,* February 21, 2000, as one in a series of "remarkable prose" pieces remembered by the editors.

It was the miracle God had wrought. And it was patently the sort of thing that could only happen once. Mechanically uncanny, it was like nothing that had ever come to the world before. Flourishing industries rose and fell with it. As a vehicle, it was hard-working, commonplace, heroic; and it often seemed to transmit those qualities to the persons who rode in it.

—"Farewell, My Lovely," ca. 1936; *Essays of E. B. White,* p. 162, and *Farewell to Model T; From Sea to Shining Sea,* pp. 16–17.

My definition of a touring car is a five- or seven-passenger low-sided open car with no glass in it except the windshield and maybe a couple of old White Rock bottles.

—"Department of Correction, Amplification, and Abuse," March 6, 1937; *The New Yorker.*

Furthermore, nobody can call a convertible an "open car" as long as the top makes a solid canopy over the rear seat, like an English pram, with not even a peak hole to look out of. The Buick which I exposed myself to in your salesroom was about as open as the back room of a 1928 speakeasy.

—"Department of Correction, Amplification, and Abuse," March 6, 1937; *The New Yorker.*

A car capable of going ninety miles an hour should give the driver every break as to vision, instead of shutting him up in a sort of hen coop.

—"Department of Correction, Amplification, and Abuse," March 6, 1937; *The New Yorker.*

The thing that would benefit New York, or any other city, would be a cab that is properly designed to fulfill the special function it has to perform. These cabs are not so designed. They are simply slight modifications of pleasure cars—and a pleasure car is about the poorest object you could get, as a model. Taxicabs are long and low because for thirty years automobile manufacturers have been boasting of long, low cars. I have personally measured the opening (vertical distance) of a cab door. It is roughly 38 inches. A taxicab is the only thing I know of that expects its patron to enter and leave by an opening 38 inches high. If you had to enter your apartment, your subway, your saloon, your bank vault, or your hall closet through a 38 inch opening, you would be infuriated, and would rebel.

—Letter to Harold Ross, January?, 1950; *Letters of E. B. White*, Rev. Ed., pp. 292–293.

Autumn
(see Seasons)

Awards

It is deeply satisfying to win a prize in front of a lot of people.
—*Charlotte's Web*, 1952, p. 160.

This, by the way, is the time of year we get fairly bitter about the honorary (uh huh) degrees* that universities confer on illustrious citizens. Not all universities are guilty of this prestige-swapping ritual, but most of them are.... When we observe a university handing out honorary degrees, we suspect it of about the same motives as those of Arthur Schreiber, the aerial stowaway; we suspect it of wanting to get in on something.

 —From "Notes and Comment," June 29, 1929; *The New Yorker.*

  * In 1948, White accepted honorary degrees from Dartmouth, Yale, and University of Maine, and others were awarded him in later years.

It was kind of you to write me about the Presidential Medal of Freedom. I was awfully sorry that I was unable to be on hand for the presentation, and to meet you there. I know President Kennedy must have approached the freedom award list as he approached everything else—with personal concern, lively interest, and knowledge. To find myself on his list was the most gratifying thing that ever happened to me, as well as a matter of pride and sober resolve. The accomplishments of presidents in office are usually measured in rather exact terms, but your brother gave the country something immeasurable and almost indescribable, for which we all will be forever grateful.

 —Letter to Robert F. Kennedy, December 24, 1963; *Letters of E. B. White,* Rev. Ed., p. 465.

Being a medalist at last, I can now speak of the "corpus" of my work—the word has a splendid sound. But glancing at the skimpy accomplishments of recent years, I find the "cadaver of my work" a more fitting phrase.

 —"The Egg Is All," *New York Times,* December 7, 1971; remarks on receiving the National Medal for Literature, The E. B.

White Collection, Carl A. Kroch Library, Cornell University, Ithaca, NY.

My Norwich Terrier will be seven in May. His Club name is Jaysgreen Rusty (United Kingdom), and he was sired (it says here) by a dog named Hunston Horseradish. He is known in this house as Jones and is seldom found more than six feet from where I am....But he and I are enough alike so that we get on well, and I can't help being touched by his loyalty—which I think in his case is simply insecurity. He would never take a prize at a show. Neither would I, come to think of it.

—Letter to Philip Hewes, March 20, 1974; *Letters of E. B. White,* Rev. Ed., p. 605.

Thanks for your congratulatory note on my Pulitzer citation. Even at my age, I'd be glad to swap off with you and be asked to crown a beauty queen.

—Letter to Hon. Edmund S. Muskie, May 1, 1978; *Letters of E. B. White,* Rev. Ed., p. 621.

Yes, Katharine would have been pleased with my Pulitzer award, and life without her is no bargain for me, awards or no awards. She was the one great award of my life and I am in awe of having received it. I find life difficult without her, not just because she helped me in so many practical ways but because she steadied me day and night, and I now feel unsteady all the time as well as untidy. I can't seem to keep up with the events of the day, or the contents of my mail sack.

—Letter to Gluyas Williams, May 8, 1978; *Letters of E. B. White,* Rev. Ed., p. 621.

Babies

Some day when I'm out of sight
Travel far but travel light!
Stalk the turtle on the log,
Watch the heron spear the frog,
Find the things you only find
When you leave your bag behind;
Raise the sail your old man furled,
Hang your hat upon the world!...

>—"Apostrophe to a Pram Rider"* (excerpt from "The Conning
> Tower"), 1931; *E. B. White: A Biography,* by Scott Elledge, p. 179.
>> * The pram rider here was White's baby son Joel, born in 1930,
>> and Joel did, indeed, grow up to "Raise the sail [his] old man
>> furled..." when he became a naval architect and boatbuilder.

Hold a baby to your ear
As you would a shell:
Sounds of centuries you hear
New centuries foretell.

Who can break a baby's code?
And which is the older—
The listener or his small load?
The held or the holder?

>—"Conch" (in its entirety), April 24, 1948; *Poems and Sketches of
> E. B. White,* 1981, p. 100.

Barn
(see also Country Life, Farming)

I am always humbled by the infinite ingenuity of the Lord, who can make a red barn cast a blue shadow.

—"A Winter Diary," 1941; *One Man's Meat*, p. 170.

When a barn eclipses a house, and a housewife begins to go to work on it, buy her a fur coat or some lily bulbs and make her leave the barn alone. Then when haying time comes around, or somebody gives you a bull calf, or it is time to set a hen, you will have the proper facilities for these maneuvers and won't find the hen sitting on ping-pong balls and the calf occupying a corner of a modern-art exhibit. There is no more satisfying structure in the whole world than a well-built old American barn, just as she stands.

—"Notes and Comment," December 5, 1953; *The New Yorker*.

I just want to add that there is no symbolism in "Charlotte's Web." And there is no political meaning in the story. It is a straight report from the barn cellar, which I dearly love, having spent so many fine hours there, winter and summer, spring and fall, good times and bad times, with the garrulous geese, the passage of swallows, the nearness of rats, and the sameness of sheep.

—Letter to Gene Deitch,* January 12, 1971; *Letters of E. B. White*, Rev. Ed., p. 563.

　　* Deitch was director of the film version of *Charlotte's Web* for Sagittarius Productions.

The barn is a community of rugged individualists, everybody mildly suspicious of everybody else, including me. Friendships sometimes develop, as between a goat and a horse, but there is no sense of true

community or cooperation. Heaven forfend! Joy of life, yes. Tolerance
of other cultures, yes. Community, no.

>   —Letter to Gene Deitch,* January 12, 1971; *Letters of E. B. White,*
>   Rev. Ed., p. 563.

>> * Deitch was going to be director of the film version of "Char-
>> lotte's Web" for Sagittarius Productions. In a November 17,
>> 1970 letter to his agent, Milton Greenstein, White had writ-
>> ten, "I feel fairly happy about Deitch—happy as I can ever be
>> in never-never land, which still gives me the shakes."—*Letters*
>> *of E. B. White,* Rev. Ed., p. 557.

Bees

When the air is wine and the wind is free
And the morning sits on the lovely lea
And sunlight ripples on every tree,
Then love-in-air is the thing for me—
I'm a bee,
I'm a ravishing, rollicking, young queen bee,
That's me.

>   —From "Song of the Queen Bee" (first stanza), December 15,
>   1945; *Second Tree from the Corner,* p. 204, and *Poems and Sketches of*
>   *E. B. White,* 1981, p. 192.

I can't afford to be too choosy;
In every queen there's a touch of floozy...

>   —From "Song of the Queen Bee" (first stanza), December 15,
>   1945; *Second Tree from the Corner,* p. 204, and *Poems and Sketches of*
>   *E. B. White,* 1981, p. 193.

Sorry to report that the situation among bees has changed since I wrote the poem.* The scientists won, and queens have been inseminated artificially, The drone not only isn't in the air, he's not even conscious—they knock him out with CO_2. Ah, progress!

  —Letter to Miriam L. Richmond, May 1, 1951; *Letters of E. B. White*, Rev. Ed., pp. 305–306.

  * The poem was titled "Song of the Queen Bee."

Biography

Congratulations on your manly attempt to make me into a literary character. It isn't going to work, but it makes great reading. I was in stitches much of the way, recalling my Early Ineptitude, my Early Sorrows, my Immaculate Romancing. What a mess I was! No wonder my father worried about me.

  —Letter to Scott Elledge,* May 25, 1982; *Letters of E. B. White*, Rev. Ed., p. 648.

  * Scott Elledge was the author of *E. B. White: A Biography.*

Quite simply the best in-depth study ever made of an out-of-his-depth man.* Hilarious.

  —Letter to Scott Elledge, May 28, 1983; *Letters of E. B. White*, Rev. Ed., p. 665.

  * White was offering his biographer a mock jacket blurb for *E. B. White: A Biography.*

The man* who is writing my biography is in worse shape than I am. He has pulmonary trouble and is worried because he picked the wrong person to write a biography about. After all, I'm no Norman Mailer, with his seven wives and occasional knifings. Nobody in his right mind would pick me for the subject of a biography.

—Letter to Ann Honeycutt, June 12, 1983; *Letters of E. B. White*, Rev. Ed., p. 665

* Scott Elledge.

I know how hard it is to write about a fellow who spends most of his time crouched over a typewriter. That was my fate, too.

—Letter to Scott Elledge, February 10, 1984; *Letters of E. B. White*, Rev. Ed., p. 677.

Birds
(see also Chickens, Egg)

Birds have their love—and—mating song,
Their warning cry, their hating song:
Some have a night song, some a day song,
A lilt, a tilt, a come–what–may song:
Birds have their careless bough and teeter song
And, of course, their Roger Tory Peter song.

—"A Listener's Guide to the Birds (After a Binge with Roger Tory Peterson in His Famous Guidebook)," July 4, 1959; *The New Yorker*.

Canada Jay
Canada jays have been observed in the vicinity, and they managed to get into the paper, under the headline "UNUSUAL BIRD SEEN." I felt pretty good about this, because I had spotted two of these

whiskey-jacks (not to be confused with cheap-Jacks) way back in October.

> —"Home-Coming," December 10, 1955; *Points of My Compass*, p. 33, and *Essays of E. B. White*, p. 11.

The Canada jay looks as though he had slept in his clothes.

> —"Home-Coming," December 10, 1955; *Points of My Compass*, p. 35, and *Essays of E. B. White*, p. 13.

Chickadee

The chickadee likes to pronounce his name;
It's extremely helpful and adds to his fame.
But in spring you can get the heebie-jeebies
Untangling chickadees from phoebes.
The chickadee, when he's all afire,
Whistles, "Fee-bee," to explain desire.
He should be arrested and thrown in jail
For impersonating another male.
  (There's a way you can tell which bird is which,
  But just the same, it's a nasty switch.)
Our gay deceiver may fancy-free be
But he never does fool a female phoebe.

> —"A Listener's Guide to the Birds (After a Binge with Roger Tory Peterson in His Famous Guidebook)," July 4, 1959; *The New Yorker.*

Crow

What answer maketh the crow?
Always "No."

Put several questions in a row
To a crow,

You will get "No, no, no,"
Or "No, no, no, no."

Sometimes, on being questioned,
The crow says, "Naw"
Or "Caw"
But regardless of pronunciation,
There is never anything but opposition, denial,
And negation
In a crow.
> —"The Answer Is No" (excerpt), December 20, 1952; *Poems and Sketches of E. B. White*, 1981, p. 111.

Geese

Geese, we have found, are alert and articulate and they practically never sleep, but they are also undiscriminating, gossipy, and as easily diverted as children.
> —"Comment," March 21, 1953; *The New Yorker*.

Any sort of disturbance, whether man-made or elemental, is of immense interest to a goose, and geese watch the world through eyes that often seem capable of seeing things not visible to men. I have always envied a goose its look of deep, superior wisdom. I miss the cordiality of geese, the midnight cordiality. And they are the world's best drinkers, forever at it.
> —Postscript to "The Eye of Edna," April 1962; *Points of My Compass*, p. 14.

Junco

Even the drabbest yardscape achieves something like elegance when a junco alights in the foreground—a beautifully turned-out little character who looks as though he were on his way to an afternoon wedding.

—"Winter Back Yard," March 24, 1951; *The New Yorker* and *Writings from* The New Yorker, *1925–1976*, p. 8.

Robin

I'm the father of two robins and this has kept me on the go lately. They were in a nest in a vine on the garage and had been deserted by their parents, and without really thinking what I was doing I casually dropped a couple of marinated worms into their throats as I walked by a week ago Monday. This did it. They took me on with open hearts and open mouths, and my schedule became extremely tight.

—Letter to Roger Angell, June 24, 1964; *Letters of E. B. White*, Rev. Ed., p. 475.

Sparrow

At this season the sparrows are particularly conspicuous because they are in love—and love addles any creature and makes him noisy.

—"Interview with a Sparrow," April 9, 1927; *Writings from* The New Yorker, *1925–1976*, p. 191.

Swallow

Swallows, I have noticed, never use any feather but a white one in their nest-building, and they always leave a lot of it showing, which makes me believe that they are interested not in the feather's insulating power but in its reflecting power, so that when they skim into the dark barn from the bright outdoors they will have a beacon to steer by.

—"Home-Coming," December 10, 1955; *Points of My Compass*, p. 34, and *Essays of E. B. White*, p. 12.

Despite the great blizzard of April,* the swallows arrived on schedule
and are busy remodeling the mud nests in the barn.

— "Introduction," May 1982; *One Man's Meat*, p. xiii.

* April 1982.

Whiskey-jack

The whiskey-jack showed up again around here a couple of years ago.
I encountered him down in the cedar swamp in the pasture, where I had
gone to look for a fox's den. The bird, instead of showing alarm at my
intrusion, followed me about, jumping silently from branch to branch in
the thick woods, seemingly eager to learn what I was up to. I found it
spooky yet agreeable to be tailed by a bird, and a disreputable one at that.

— "Home-Coming," December 10, 1955; *Points of My Compass*,
pp. 34–35, and *Essays of E. B. White*, pp. 12–13.

She* even built for my pleasure a new bird bath, only bird bath in
America that is located on top of the septic tank. (She doesn't remember
where the tank is, But *I* do, because I had to exhume it last year in order
to check the backup of sewage into the shower bath. The bird bath has
a statue of St. Francis worked into the scheme, and if the plumbing goes
on the blink again, I'll have to start by dismantling a saint....)

— Letter to Allene White, January 15, 1964; *Letters of E. B. White*,
Rev. Ed., p. 466.

* A landlady in Sarasota, Florida.

Wren

"My name is Margalo," said the bird, softly, in a musical voice.
"I come from fields once tall with wheat, from pastures deep in fern
and thistle; I come from vales of meadowsweet, and I love to whistle."

— *Stuart Little*, 1945, p. 51.

Boats and Boating
(see also Sea)

It never has been hard for me
    To quit my duties clerical
And take my passage on the sea
    Where things are blue and spherical.
I leave the sane and stable shore
    To learn a ship's propensities,
And standing aft or standing fore
    I ponder the immensities.
     —"Navigation" (excerpt), July 14, 1928; *The New Yorker.*

I became a pelagic boy. The sea became my unspoken challenge: the wind, the tide, the fog, the ledge, the bell, the gull that cried help, the never-ending threat and bluff of weather. Once having permitted the wind to enter the belly of my sail, I was not able to quit the helm; it was as though I had seized hold of a high-tension wire and could not let go.
    —"The Sea and the Wind That Blows," 1963; *Essays of E. B. White,*
        p. 206.

I liked to sail alone. The sea was the same as a girl to me—I did not want anyone else along. Lacking instruction, I invented ways of getting things done, and usually ended by doing them in a rather queer fashion, and so did not learn to sail properly, and still cannot sail well, although I have been at it all my life. I was twenty before I discovered that charts existed; all my navigating up to that time was done with the wariness and the ignorance of the early explorers.
    —"The Sea and the Wind That Blows," 1963; *Essays of E. B. White,*
        p. 206.

The ideal instructor in weather is not a studio prophet but a sail-boat, which draws its nourishment from the wind and develops in the helmsman a wariness that is part respect and part pleasurable anticipation of bold encounter.

—"Notes and Comment," June 18, 1955; *The New Yorker.*

Over the pond the west wind blew, and into the teeth of the west wind sailed the sloops and schooners, their rails well down, their wet decks gleaming. The owners, boys and grown men, raced around the cement shores hoping to arrive at the other side in time to keep the boats from bumping. Some of the toy boats were not as small as you might think, for when you got close to them you found that their mainmast was taller than a man's head, and they were beautifully made, with everything shipshape and ready for sea. To Stuart they seemed enormous, and he hoped he would be able to get aboard one of them and sail away to the far corners of the pond. (He was an adventurous little fellow and loved the feel of the breeze in his face and the cry of the gulls overhead and the heave of the great swell under him.)

—*Stuart Little,* 1945, pp. 30–31.

"That's the Lillian B. Womrath," said the man, "and I hate her with all my heart."

"Then so do I," cried Stuart, loyally.

"I hate her because she is always bumping into my boat," continued the man, "and because her owner is a lazy boy who doesn't understand sailing and who hardly knows a squall from a squid."

"Or a jib from a jibe," cried Stuart.

"Or a luff from a leech," bellowed the man.

"Or a deck from a dock," screamed Stuart.

"Or a mast from a mist," yelled the man.

—*Stuart Little,* 1945, p. 33.

This morning made preparations for building a boat—the first boat I ever prepared to build.* Bought ten cents' worth of wicking and borrowed some caulking tools, and prepared myself further by asking a man how to build a boat and he told me. It is to be a small scow, made of native cedar.... All morning at work boat-building. Had a stove going in the shop and, although it was a cold rainy morning, all was cheerful inside. The cedar shavings smell good and are worth the effort of planing. The boat has been named *Flounder*. I am perfectly happy doing anything of this sort and would rather construct something than do any other sort of work. When I needed a three-eighth inch dowel stick I had to dismast a small American flag and use the staff, but it worked well and is now an integral part of *Flounder*.

    —"The Wave of the Future," 1940; *One Man's Meat*, p. 164.

     * White's son Joel was about to turn ten and the scow, modeled on one from the *American Boy's Handy Book*, was his first boat. Joel later became a naval architect and boatyard owner in Maine.

My boy loved our rented outboard, and his great desire was to achieve single-handed mastery over it, and authority, and he soon learned the trick of choking it a little (but not too much), and the adjustment of the needle valve. Watching him, I would remember the things you could do with the old one-cylinder engine with the heavy flywheel, how you could have it eating out of your hand if you got really close to it spiritually.

    —"Once More to the Lake," August 1941; *Essays of E. B. White*, p. 201.

Motorboats in those days didn't have clutches, and you would make a landing by shutting off the motor at the proper time and coasting in with a dead rudder. But there was a way of reversing them, if you learned the trick, by cutting the switch and putting it on again exactly on the final dying revolution of the flywheel, so that it would kick back against compression and begin reversing. Approaching a dock in a strong following breeze, it was difficult to slow up sufficiently by the ordinary coasting method, and if a boy felt he had complete mastery over his motor, he was tempted to keep it running beyond its time and then reverse it a few feet from the dock. It took a cool nerve, because if you threw the switch a twentieth of a second too soon you would catch the flywheel when it still had speed enough to go up past center, and the boat would leap ahead, charging bull-fashion at the dock.

—"Once More to the Lake," August 1941; *Essays of E. B. White*,
p. 201.

A good boat, strongly built and well maintained, doesn't depreciate greatly in value, as a car does, and a man may wait thirty years to realize his dream, only to find that by the time he is wealthy enough to buy the boat, he has become too emaciated to hoist sail and get the anchor.

—"Boat Shows," January 19, 1952; *Writings from* The New Yorker,
1925–1976, p. 219.

A man feels about a boat entirely differently from the way he feels about a car: he falls in love with it, often from afar, and the affair is a secret one—comparable to that of a young girl who sleeps with an actor's photograph under her pillow.

—"Boat Shows," January 19, 1952; *Writings from* The New Yorker,
1925–1976, p. 219.

Dear Hum: My son, who is a boat designer, designed a punt for a man and asked me to think of a name for it. Quick as a flash, I gave him Punt of No Return. Thought you should know about this. Love, Ho*

—Unpublished letter to Howard Baker Cushman, June 7, 1953; The E. B. White Collection, Carl A. Kroch Library, Cornell University, Ithaca, NY.

* In 1922, Howard Cushman had traveled across the country in a Model T with White, both of them free lancing to earn gas money. White later published book collections of *New Yorker* "newsbreaks" under the titles *Ho-Hum* and *Another Ho-Hum.*

Waking or sleeping, I dream of boats—usually of rather small boats under a slight press of sail.

—"The Sea and the Wind That Blows," 1963; *Essays of E. B. White,* p. 205.

If a man must be obsessed by something, I suppose a boat is as good as anything, perhaps a bit better than most. A small sailing craft is not only beautiful, it is seductive and full of strange promise and the hint of trouble.

—"The Sea and the Wind That Blows," 1963; *Essays of E. B. White,* p. 205.

Men who ache all over for tidiness and compactness in their lives often find relief for their pain in the cabin of a thirty-foot sailboat at anchor in a sheltered cove. Here the sprawling panoply of The Home is compressed in orderly miniature and liquid delirium, suspended between the bottom of the sea and the top of the sky, ready to move on in the morning by the miracle of canvas and the witchcraft of rope. It is small wonder that men hold boats in the secret place of their mind, almost from the cradle to the grave.

—"The Sea and the Wind That Blows," 1963; *Essays of E. B. White,* pp. 205–206.

And with the tiller in my hand, I'll feel again the wind imparting life to a boat, will smell again the old menace, the one that imparts life to me: the cruel beauty of the salt world, the barnacle's tiny knives, the sharp spine of the urchin, the stinger of the sun jelly, the claw of the crab.

—"The Sea and the Wind That Blows," 1963; *Essays of E. B. White*, p. 207.

Books
(see also Reading)

A book should be the occasion of rejoicing, but it is seldom that, imparting a feeling of completion but not of satisfaction.

—"Foreword," *Second Tree from the Corner*, p. xiv.

I feel like the millionth person through a turnstile—dazed and happy. Dear me, 100,000 books! It's a little indecent, isn't it? ... When I recover from my 100,000th head cold, which is now upon me, I'd like to take you to Milestone Luncheon at some fashionable restaurant, in celebration. You can eat 100,000 stalks of celery, and I'll swallow 100,000 olives. It will be the E. B. White-Ursula Nordstrom* Book and Olive luncheon.

—Letter to Ursula Nordstrom, December 17, 1946; *Letters of E. B. White*, Rev. Ed., pp. 261–262.

* Ursula Nordstrom was head of Harper Junior Books and later a senior editor at Harper & Row Publishers. She had written White to say that 100,000 copies of *Stuart Little* had sold. (Current sales are well over four million, excluding foreign sales.) The luncheon took place at the Algonquin and White gave Nordstrom a jar of caviar with the note: "Guaranteed to contain 100,000 sturgeon eggs ... Spread them in health!"

All that I hope to say in books, all that I ever* hope to say, is that I love the world. I guess you can find that in there, if you dig around.

—Unpublished letter to a *Charlotte's Web* reader; quoted in *The Annotated Charlotte's Web* and *E. B. White, A Biography*, pp. 300–301.

* The quotation about loving the world was written in response to a reader who was asking about the "meaning of *Charlotte's Web*." White realized that some readers want to assign symbolism to his works, a trend that he resisted; if you listen between the lines you may hear a hint of pique: "all that I *ever* hope to say."

Cancer

Under separate cover I have dispatched a contribution...to the American Cancer Society. I have been supporting the Society for many years, having lost a mother and sister to cancer,* and I have often wondered whether the Society is spending its money in the best possible way. Most of the money, I gather, goes to research on a *cure* for cancer, and so far there isn't any. Much of the money, it seems to me, should go to lobbying against the damned chemicals and pesticides and fungicides and additives and preservatives that *cause* cancer. Everybody knows they do.

—Letter to Bill ___, May 10, 1978; *Letters of E. B. White*, Rev. Ed., p. 622.

* E. B. White's son Joel McCoun White (1930–1997), also died of cancer.

Capitalism
(see Commerce)

Chickens
(see also Birds, Egg)

Chickens do not always enjoy an honorable position among city-bred people, although the egg, I notice, goes on and on. Right now the egg is in favor. The war has deified her and she is the darling of the home front, feted at conference tables, praised in every smoking car, her girlish ways and curious habits the topic of many an excited husband-ryman to whom yesterday she was a stranger without honor or allure.
    —"Introduction," *A Basic Chicken Guide for the Small Flock Owner,* by Roy E. Jones, p. v.

Here, then, is my Basic Chicken Guide: Be tidy. Be brave. Elevate all laying house feeders and waterers twenty-two inches off the floor....Walk, don't run. Never carry any strange objects into the henhouse with you.
    —"Introduction," *A Basic Chicken Guide for the Small Flock Owner,* by Roy E. Jones, p. vi.

Don't try to convey your enthusiasm for chickens to anyone else.
    —"Introduction," *A Basic Chicken Guide for the Small Flock Owner,* by Roy E. Jones, p. vi.

Keep Rocks if you are a nervous man, Reds if you are a quiet one. Don't drop shingle nails on a brooder house floor....Do all your thinking and planning backwards, starting with a sold egg, ending with a boughten starter. Don't keep chickens if you don't like chickens, or even if you don't like chicken manure. Always count your chickens before they are hatched.
    —"Introduction," *A Basic Chicken Guide for the Small Flock Owner,* by Roy E. Jones, p. vi.

A common charge made against the hen is that she is a silly creature. It is a false charge. A hen is an alarmist but she is not silly. She has a strong sense of disaster, but many of her fears seem to me well founded: I have seen inexperienced people doing things around hens which, if I were a hen, would alarm me, too.

—"Introduction," *A Basic Chicken Guide for the Small Flock Owner,* by Roy E. Jones, p. vii.

If chickens are to be merely a luxury or a fad, and you have money in your pants and want to erect a dream palace for hens and hire a governess to look after their wants and button them up, then that is a different story; but I am sure it is neither patriotic nor sensible to keep hens extravagantly or ineptly, or at too great cost in materials and time.

—"Introduction," *A Basic Chicken Guide for the Small Flock Owner,* by Roy E. Jones, pp. vii–viii.

[A] hen on a sad morning making her sad noise and undoing your cleverest devices, can take the stuffing out of a man about as fast as anything I know.

—"Introduction," *A Basic Chicken Guide for the Small Flock Owner,* by Roy E. Jones, p. viii.

I have had a lifetime of experience with broody hens, and if there is any more unpredictable female, I don't know what it is.

—Letter to Reginald Allen, March 5, 1973; *Letters of E. B. White,* Rev. Ed., p. 591.

Childhood
(see also Aging, Youth)

I have heard it said that rats collect trinkets, that if you expose a rat's nest, you may find bright bits of glass and other small desirable objects. A child's mind is such a repository—full of gems of questionable merit, paste and real, held in storage.

—"Children's Books," November, 1938; *One Man's Meat*, p. 22.

Children pay better attention than grownups.

—*Charlotte's Web* (spoken by Dr. Dorian), 1952, p. 110.

Children, it seems to us, start life with an open mind about the weather; left to their own devices, they accept rain with stoical calm (as do animals) and greet snow with positive delight.

—"Notes and Comment," June 18, 1955; *The New Yorker.*

These were the pleasantest days of Sam's life, these days in the woods, far, far from everywhere—no automobiles, no roads, no people, no noise, no school, no homework, no problems, except the problem of getting lost. And, of course, the problem of what to be when he grew up. Every boy has *that* problem.

—*Trumpet of the Swan*, 1970, p. 4.

As a very small boy, I used to repair to the cellar, where I would pee in the coal bin—for variety.

—"Mount Vernon," 1976; *Letters of E. B. White*, Rev. Ed., p. 2.

Christmas

To perceive Christmas through its wrapping becomes more difficult with every year.

—"The Distant Music of the Hounds," 1954; *Second Tree from the Corner*, p. 131, and *Notes on Our Times*, p. 109.

The miracle of Christmas is that, like the distant and very musical voice of the hound, it penetrates finally and becomes heard in the heart—over so many years, through so many cheap curtain-raisers.

    —"The Distant Music of the Hounds," 1954; *Second Tree from the Corner*, p. 132, and *Notes on Our Times*, p. 109.

This week, many will be reminded that no explosion of atoms generates so hopeful a light as the reflection of a star, seen appreciatively in a pasture pond. It is there we perceive Christmas—and the sheep quiet, and the world waiting.

    —"The Distant Music of the Hounds," 1954; *Second Tree from the Corner*, p. 133, and *Notes on Our Times*, p. 112.

In line with the government's policy of altering the dates of holidays to give people more time for rest and recreation, we have a suggestion for one more change. Christmas should be switched from December 25th to February 29th. This would provide a decent interval between our spells of national hysteria, stem the tide of inflation, restore millions of American males to a state of health, build the character of the nation's children in accordance with President Nixon's ideal of discipline and responsibility, take women out of the stores and put them back in the home and the office, and usher in a new era of tranquility, sanity, and peace.

    —"The Talk of the Town," December 2, 1972; *The New Yorker*.

City Life
(see also Country Life, New York City)

One qualification of a doorman is that he be unbending. A deviation of more than two inches from the perpendicular injures a doorman in a physical way, long uprightness having made him brittle. But when snow comes to the city, it falls softly on the heads of doormen, the same as on other folk; and it also falls at the feet of doormen, and accumulates there. During a recent snowfall we saw a handsome fellow, all gold braid and sparkle, shoveling the sidewalk. It was duty, and he was duty-bound—to shovel and to bend.

—"Notes and Comment," March 17, 1928; *The New Yorker.*

Many tell us that the cities are dying; and if the cities die, it will be the same as Man's own death.

—"The Egg Is All," *New York Times,* December 7, 1971; remarks on receiving the National Medal for Literature.

"How are you going to keep from getting provincial?" asked one of our friends quite solemnly. It was such a sudden question, I couldn't think of any answer, so just let it go. But afterward I wondered how my friend, on his part, was going to keep from getting metropolitan.

—"How Weather," July, 1939; *One Man's Meat,* p. 72.

The urban scene is a spectacle that fascinates me. People are animals, and the city is full of people in strange plumage, defending their territorial rights, digging for their supper.

—"The Art of the Essay, No. I, E. B. White," interview with George A. Plimpton and Frank H. Crowther, Fall 1969; *Paris Review,* Issue 48.

College
(see also Education)

Up early this day, trying to decide whether or not to bequeath our brain to our alma mater, which is making a collection of such stuff. It struck us as odd that the decision will have to be made by the brain itself and that no other part of us—a foot or a gall bladder—can be in on the matter, although all are, in a way, concerned. Our head is small and we fear that our brain may suffer by comparison if arranged on a shelf with others. Spent part of the morning composing an inscription to go with our brain, but all we got was this:

Observe, quick friend, this quiet noodle,

The kit removed from its caboodle.

Here sits a brain at last unhinged,

On which too many thoughts impinged.

—"Daylight and Darkness; *Second Tree from the Corner*, p. 127, and *Poems and Sketches of E. B. White*, p. 186.

I've never been an administrator, never been a member of a faculty, never been under fire. It's not easy to keep the true dissenters (those who want to improve something) separate from the phony dissenters (those who want to destroy the whole business). The two intermingle in the heat of campus controversy.

—"E. B. White: Notes and Comment by Author," interview with Israel Shenker, July 11, 1969; *New York Times*.

Universities have become very big, and with the bigness comes remoteness, inaccessibility. This is bad, and it causes trouble. When I was an undergraduate, there were a few professors who went out of their way to befriend students. At the house of one of these men I felt more at home than I did in my own home with my own mother and father. I felt excited, instructed, accepted, influential, and in a healthy condition. Apparently, most students today don't enjoy any such experience, and they are ready to dismantle the Establishment before they have either defined it or tasted it. In a democracy, dissent is as essential as the air we breathe. It's only when students form an elite society, immune from ordinary restraints, that I worry about dissent.

—"E. B. White: Notes and Comment by Author," interview with Israel Shenker, July 11, 1969; *New York Times*.

Returning to the college town
And sitting in the room,
I saw the neatly folded hills,
I heard the blessing of the bells;
And looking south and looking west
Watching the light that crowned the hills,
I waited to be blessed.

—"Incident on a Campus" (first stanza), *Poems and Sketches of E. B. White*, 1981, p. 109.

Commerce

There's no doubt that the profit system is thoroughly disreputable. But so is an old pair of shoes; we sort of hate to throw them away, they fit so good.

—"The Talk of the Town," June 9, 1934; *The New Yorker*.

Commuter—one who spends his life
In riding to and from his wife;
A man who shaves and takes a train
And then rides back to shave again.

—"Commuter," October 24, 1925; *The New Yorker* and *The Lady Is Cold*, p. 31.

Advertisers are the interpreters of our dreams—Joseph interpreting for Pharaoh. Like the movies, they infect the routine futility of our days with purposeful adventure. Their weapons are our weaknesses: fear, ambition, illness, pride, selfishness, desire, ignorance. And these weapons must be kept as bright as a sword.

——"Truth in Advertising," July 11, 1936; *The New Yorker*.

Some day, if I ever get around to it, I would like to write the definitive review of America's most fascinating book, the Sears Roebuck catalogue. It is a monumental volume, and in many households is a more powerful document than the Bible. It makes living in the country not only practical but a sort of perpetual night-before-Christmas.

——"Second World War," September, 1939; *One Man's Meat*, p. 84.

The device of withholding tax money, which is clearly confiscatory, since the individual is not allowed to see, taste, or touch a certain percentage of his wages, tacitly brands him as negligent or unthrifty or immature or incompetent or dishonest, or all of those things at once.

——"Withholding," February 5, 1944; *Second Tree from the Corner*, p. 124, and *Notes on Our Times*, p. 78.

I think there is a certain stubborn streak in automakers. They were slow to give up the gas-guzzling car in favor of a more sensible vehicle. They seem to want every car to be either a Cadillac or a poor man's dream of a Cadillac. But of course there have been a lot of innovative cars come onto the market—the minibuses and the vans and the campers. Vogue is still a strong influence in the industry, and vogue is responsible for a lot of accidents that never need have occurred.

——Letter to Mr. Laffoon, *Detroit Free Press Magazine*, April 12, 1980; *Letters of E. B. White*, Rev. Ed., p. 633.

Common Sense

One nation's common sense is another nation's high blood pressure.
   —*The Wild Flag,* August 12, 1944, p. 33.

The sense that is common to one generation is uncommon to the next.
   —"The Ring of Time," March 22, 1956; *Points of My Compass,*
   p. 58, and *Essays of E. B. White,* p. 148.

The only sense that is common, in the long run, is the sense of
change—and we all instinctively avoid it, and object to the passage of
time, and would rather have none of it.
   —"The Ring of Time," March 22, 1956; *Points of My Compass,*
   pp. 58–59, and *Essays of E. B. White,* p. 148.

Counsel

Never hurry and never worry!
   —*Charlotte's Web* (spoken by Charlotte), 1952, p. 64.

Keep fit, and don't lose your nerve.
   —*Charlotte's Web* (spoken by Charlotte), 1952, p. 64.

Sleep is important.
   —*Charlotte's Web* (spoken by Charlotte), 1952, p. 64.

Sleep, sleep, my love, my only,
Deep, deep, in the dung and the dark;
Be not afraid and be not lonely!

This is the hour when frogs and thrushes
Praise the world from the woods and rushes.
Rest from care, my one and only,
Deep in the dung and the dark!
　　—*Charlotte's Web* (Charlotte's lullaby for Wilbur the pig), 1952,
　　p. 104.

Country Life
(see also Barn, City Life, Farming, Maine)

Even doing everything all wrong in the country is fun.
　　—"Notes and Comment," December 5, 1953; *The New Yorker*.

Whenever I tell about spring, or any delights that I experience, or
the pleasant country, I think of a conversation I had with a friend
in the city shortly before I left. "I trust," he said with an ugly leer,
"that you will spare the reading public your little adventures in
contentment."
　　—"Spring," April, 1941; *One Man's Meat*, pp. 188–189.

As a man in the country, I have had my old friends in town to reckon
with, most of whom regard the hen as a comic prop straight out of
vaudeville. When I would return to city haunts for a visit, these friends
would greet me with a patronizing little smile and the withering question: "How are all the chickens?" Their scorn only increased my de-
votion to the hen. I remained loyal, as a man would to a bride whom
his family received with open ridicule. Now it is my turn to wear the
smile, as I listen to the enthusiastic cackling of urbanites, who have
suddenly taken up the hen socially and who fill the air with their

newfound ecstasy and knowledge and the relative charms of the New Hampshire Red and the Laced Wyandotte.

—"Introduction," *A Basic Chicken Guide for the Small Flock Owner,* by Roy E. Jones, p. v.

Countless persons have had disastrous experiences with chickens— city persons who have imagined they could retire to the country and, with no previous training and no particular aptitude, make a nice living with hens. They might better have chosen dancing bears.

—"Introduction," *A Basic Chicken Guide for the Small Flock Owner,* by Roy E. Jones, p. vii.

I discovered, though, that once having given a pig an enema there is no turning back, no chance of resuming one of life's more stereotyped roles. The pig's lot and mine were inextricably bound now, as though the rubber tube were the silver cord.

—"Death of a Pig," Autumn, 1947; *Essays of E. B. White,* p. 21.

A wood stove is like a small boat; it costs something to keep, but it satisfies a man's dream life.

—"Coon Tree," June 14, 1956; *Points of My Compass,* p. 71, and *Essays of E. B. White,* p. 42.

Courage

I looked a mountain in the face,
   And never faltered;
I put a river in its place,
   Courage unaltered;

I flew the pathways of the sky,
Mildly amused that I might die.
I thumbed my nose when clouds went by.

And then they took me, bold and glib,
To see a baby in a crib—
They led me forward, brave and grinning,
To see a person just beginning.
    I plainly saw how true it was,
    How extra small and new it was,
And there it breathed, and there it lay:
And *that* was when my knees gave way.
    —"The Courageous One" (in its entirety), March 23, 1929; *The New Yorker.*

I am much obliged (yes terribly much obliged) to you for your warm, courteous, and ept treatment of a rather weak, skinny subject.* Only here and there were you far off. I do not sail a 30 foot boat expertly. I sail one courageously—a different matter.
    —Letter to James Thurber, mid-October, 1938; *Letters of E. B. White*, Rev. Ed., p. 173.
        * A piece about White by James Thurber appeared in the *Saturday Review*, October 15, 1938.

If the "Second Tree" means anything, it merely means that courage (or reassurance) often comes very unexpectedly, and from a surprising source. For which we should all be, I guess, profoundly grateful.
    —Letter to Helen Margolis, December 22, 1954; *Letters of E. B. White*, Rev. Ed., p. 367.

Today, with so much of earth damaged and endangered, with so much of life dispiriting or joyless, a writer's courage can easily fail him. I feel this daily.

— "The Egg Is All," *New York Times*, December 7, 1971; remarks on receiving the National Medal for Literature.

Cows

My cow turned out to be a very large one. The first time I led her out I felt the way I did the first time I ever took a girl to the theater— embarrassed but elated. In both instances the female walked with a firmer step than mine, seemed rather in charge of the affair, and excited me with her sweet scent.

— "A Week in November," November, 1942; *One Man's Meat,* p. 266.

Critics

The critic leaves at curtain fall
To find, in starting to review it,
He scarcely saw the play at all
For starting to review it.

— "The Critic," October 17, 1925; *The New Yorker* and *The Lady Is Cold,* p. 51.

I can't criticize poetry, any more than I can dissect miracles, so I will fall back on what a little girl told her father. The poor guy was trying to write a review of my recent book for *Down East Magazine* and in desperation put the matter up to his 6-year-old daughter, who cleared the whole business up by saying, "It's a good story because I like it." Your poems are good because I like them.

    —Letter to Philip Booth, November 22, 1970; *Letters of E. B. White*, Rev. Ed., p. 558.

Death

I spent several days and nights in mid-September with an ailing pig and I feel driven to account for this stretch of time, more particularly since the pig died at last, and I lived, and things might easily have gone the other way round and none left to do the accounting.

    —"Death of a Pig," Autumn 1947; *Essays of E. B. White*, p. 1

When we slid the body into the grave, we both were shaken to the core. The loss we felt was not the loss of ham but the loss of pig.

    —"Death of a Pig," Autumn 1947; *Essays of E. B. White*, p. 18.

Thank you for sending me the clipping about my untimely demise. I shall post it on the bulletin board in the kitchen, to remind my cook that I am still taking nourishment. You didn't say what paper published it, but I don't suppose it makes any difference.

    —Letter to Mrs. Arlyn S. Adolf, August 2, 1979; *Letters of E. B. White*, Rev. Ed., p. 629.

The publishers of a forthcoming volume of poetry have advised us that by subscribing to it we can have our name "incorporated into the front matter of the book" along with the names of the other subscribers. This, of course, would immortalize us as a person who once read a book—or at any rate as a person who once *intended* to read a book. It is not the sort of immortality we crave, our feeling being

that deathlessness should be arrived at in a more haphazard fashion. Loving fame as much as any man, we shall carve our initials in the shell of a tortoise and turn him loose in a peat bog.
—"Immortality," March 28, 1936; *Writings from* The New Yorker, *1925–1976*, p. 223.

Democracy
(see also Government)

But as we understand it, one of the noblest attributes of democracy is that it contains no one who can truthfully say, of two pots, which is the cracked, which is the whole. That is basic.
—"No Crackpots?" September 12, 1942; *Writings from* The New Yorker, *1925–1976*, p. 137.

Democracy is the recurrent suspicion that more than half of the people are right more than half of the time.
—*The Wild Flag,* July 3, 1944, p. 31.

It is the line that forms on the right. It is the don't in Don't Shove. It is the hole in the stuffed shirt through which the sawdust slowly trickles; it is the dent in the high hat.
—*The Wild Flag,* July 3, 1944, p. 31.

It is the feeling of privacy in the voting booths, the feeling of communion in the libraries, the feeling of vitality everywhere.
—*The Wild Flag,* July 3, 1944, p. 31.

Democracy is the score at the beginning of the ninth.
—*The Wild Flag,* July 3, 1944, p. 31.

It is an idea which hasn't been disproved yet, a song the words of which have not gone bad. It's the mustard on the hot dog and the cream in the rationed coffee.

—*The Wild Flag*, July 3, 1944, p. 31.

[T]he reading room of a college library is the very temple of democracy.

—"Academic Freedom," February 26, 1949; *Writings from* The New Yorker, *1925–1976*, p. 138.

We grow tyrannical fighting tyranny. This is bad. I think the most alarming spectacle today is not the spectacle of the atomic bomb in an unfederated world, it is the spectacle of Americans beginning to accept the device of loyalty oaths and witchhunts, beginning to call anybody they don't like a Communist.

—Letter to Janice White, April 27, 1952; *Letters of E. B. White*, Rev. Ed., p. 328.

Democracy, if I understand it at all, is a society in which the unbeliever feels undisturbed and at home. If there were only half a dozen unbelievers in America, their well-being would be a test of our democracy, their tranquility would be its proof. The repeated suggestion by the present administration that religious faith is a precondition of the American way of life is disturbing to me and, I am willing to bet, to a good many other citizens.

—"A Letter from the East: Bedfellows," February 6, 1956; *Points of My Compass*, pp. 44–45, and *Essays of E. B. White*, pp. 85–86.

Democracy is itself a religious faith. For some it comes close to being the only formal religion they have. And so when I see the first faint shadow of orthodoxy sweep across the sky, feel the first cold whiff of its blinding fog steal in from sea, I tremble all over, as though I had just seen an eagle go by, carrying a baby.

—"A Letter from the East: Bedfellows," February 6, 1956; *Points of My Compass*, p. 46, and *Essays of E. B. White*, p. 86.

It should be the concern of our democracy that no child shall feel uncomfortable because of belief.* This condition cannot be met if a schoolmaster is empowered to establish a standard of religious rectitude based on a particular form of worship.

—Letter to Senator Margaret Chase Smith, August 15, 1966; *Letters of E. B. White*, Rev. Ed., p. 495.

* Re: The proposed Dirksen amendment.

Diplomacy

Diplomacy is the lowest form of politeness because it misquotes the greatest number of people. A nation, like an individual, if it has anything to say, should simply say it. This will be hard on editorial writers and news commentators, who are always glad to have diplomatic notes to interpret; but it will be better for the people.

—"Compost," June 1940; *One Man's Meat*, p. 132.

Disarmament
(see Peace, War)

Dogs

LOST—Male fox hound, brown head, yellow legs, blue body with large black spots on left side, male. Also female, white with red head and spot on hip.—*Fayette (Mo.) Democrat Leader*

Those aren't dogs, those are nasturtiums.

—Early *New Yorker* newsbreak, "Ho-Hum," p. 60.

It is not so much that I acquire dogs as it is that dogs acquire me. Maybe they even shop for me, I don't know. If they do I assume that they have many problems, because they certainly always arrive with plenty, which they then turn over to me.

—"Dog Training," November, 1940; *One Man's Meat*, p. 161.

A really companionable and indispensable dog is an accident of nature. You can't get it by breeding for it, and you can't buy it with money. It just happens along.

—"Dog Training," November, 1940; *One Man's Meat*, p. 162.

I can still see my first dog in all the moods and situations that memory has filed him away in, but I think of him oftenest as he used to be right after breakfast on the back porch, listlessly eating up a dish of petrified oatmeal rather than hurt my feelings. For six years he met me at the same place after school and convoyed me home—a service he thought up himself. A boy doesn't forget that sort of association.

—"Dog Training," November, 1940; *One Man's Meat*, p. 163.

The Dog Show is the only place I know of where you can watch a lady go down on her knees in public to show off the good points of a dog, thus obliterating her own.

—"Turtle Bay Diary," February 22, 1947; *The New Yorker*.

I have a spaniel that defrocked a nun last week. He took hold of the cord. I had hold of the leash. It was like elephants holding tails. Imagine me undressing a nun, even second hand.

—Letter to Alexander Woollcott, November 1934?; *Letters of E. B. White*, Rev. Ed., p. 114.

The dwarf pear has bark trouble. My puppy has no bark trouble. He arises at three, for tennis. The puppy's health, in fact, is exceptionally good.... I knew that as soon as the puppy reached home and got his sea legs he would switch to the supplement *du jour*—a flake of well-rotted cow manure from my boot, a dead crocus bulb from the lawn, a shingle from the kindling box, a bloody feather from the execution block behind the barn. Time has borne me out; the puppy was not long in discovering the delicious supplements of the farm, and he now knows where every vitamin hides, under its stone, under its loose board. I even introduced him to the tonic smell of coon.

—"A Report in Spring," May 10, 1957; *Points of My Compass*, pp. 112–113, and *Essays of E. B. White*, p. 15.

My dog welcomes any American, day or night, and who am I to let a dog outdo me in simple courtesy?

—"Khrushchev and I (A Study in Similarities)," September 26, 1959; *Writings from* The New Yorker, *1925–1976*, p. 100.

I wish instead I were doing what my dog is doing at this moment, rolling in something ripe he has found on the beach in order to take on its smell. His is such an easy, simple way to increase one's stature and enlarge one's personality.

—"E. B. White: Notes and Comment by Author," interview with Israel Shenker, July 11, 1969; *New York Times.*

My New Year began with a dog fight. A few minutes before midnight on New Year's Eve, Jones [a Norwich terrier] informed me that we were in imminent danger from an intruder and that we had better do something about it right away.... Jones by this time was in a terrible fury and wanted to kill the poodle. The poodle accepted the challenge, and in a jiffy I was in the vortex of a whirlpool of dog flesh that seemed to consist of about six enormous black poodles and about ten tiny Norwich terriers....French poodles are very strange when they fight—they seem to keep their cool and operate on a high intellectual plane, like Gene Tunney.

—Letter to Martha White, January 5, 1969; *Letters of E. B. White,* Rev. Ed., pp. 522–523.

Today the Boxer
Is fashionable and snappy;
But I never saw a Boxer
Who looked thoroughly happy.

—"Fashions in Dogs," December 19, 1936; *Poems and Sketches of E. B. White,* 1981, p. 151.

Dachshunds
The dachshund's affectionate,
He wants to wed with you:
Lie down to sleep.
And he's in bed with you.
Sit in a chair,
He's there.
Depart,
You break his heart.

—"Fashions in Dogs," December 19, 1936; *Poems and Sketches of E. B. White,* 1981, p. 152.

A full moon tonight, which made the dogs uneasy. First a neighbor's dog, a quarter of a mile away, felt the moon—he began shortly after dark, a persistent complaint, half longing. Then our big dog, whose supper had not sat well, took up the moonsong. I shut him in the barn where his bed is, but he kept up the barking, with an odd howl now and again; and I could hear him roaming round in there, answering the neighbor's dog and stirring up Fred, our dachshund and superintendent, who suddenly, from a deep sleep, roused up and pulled on his executive frown (as a man, waking, might hastily pull on a pair of trousers) and dashed out into the hall as through the moon were a jewel robber.

—"A Week in April," April, 1939; *One Man's Meat*, p. 47.

I like to read books on dog training. Being the owner of dachshunds, to me a book on dog discipline becomes a volume of inspired humor. Every sentence is a riot.

—"Dog Training," November, 1940; *One Man's Meat*, p. 160.

For a number of years past I have been agreeably encumbered by a very large and dissolute dachshund named Fred. Of all the dogs whom I have served I've never known one who understood so much of what I say or held it in such deep contempt. When I address Fred I never have to raise either my voice or my hopes. He even disobeys me when I instruct him in something that he wants to do. And when I answer his peremptory scratch at the door and hold the door open for him to walk through, he stops in the middle and lights a cigarette, just to hold me up.

—"Dog Training," November, 1940; *One Man's Meat*, p. 160.

As my own spirits declined, along with the pig's, the spirits of my vile old dachshund* rose. The frequency of our trips down the footpath through the orchard to the pigyard delighted him, although he suffers greatly from arthritis, moves with difficulty, and would be bedridden if he could find anyone willing to serve him meals on a tray.

—"Death of a Pig," Autumn 1947; *Essays of E. B. White*, p. 20.
 * Named Fred.

97

My advice, if you have a dachshund puppy, is to subscribe to the *New York Times*, and instead of reading it just distribute it liberally all over the house.

    —Letter to H. K. Rigg, June ?, 1950; *Letters of E. B. White*, Rev. Ed.,
        p. 295.

You have to watch out about dachshunds—some of them are as delicately balanced as a watch....

    —Letter to H. K. Rigg, June ?, 1950; *Letters of E. B. White*, Rev. Ed.,
        p. 296.

There had been talk in our family of getting a "sensible" dog this time, and my wife and I had gone over the list of sensible dogs, and had even ventured once or twice into the company of sensible dogs. A friend had a litter of Labradors, and there were other opportunities. But after a period of uncertainty and waste motion my wife suddenly exclaimed one evening, "Oh, let's just get a dachshund!" She had had a glass of wine, and I could see that the truth was coming out. Her tone was one of exasperation laced with affection. So I engaged a black male without further ado.

    —"A Report in Spring," May 10, 1957; *Points of My Compass*, p.
        111, and *Essays of E. B. White*, p. 14.

For the long ordeal of owning another dachshund we prepared ourselves by putting up for a night at the Boston Ritz in a room overlooking to Public Garden, where from our window we could gaze, perhaps for the last time, on a world of order and peace.

    —"A Report in Spring," May 10, 1957; *Points of My Compass*,
        p. 111, and *Essays of E. B. White*, p. 14.

Doom
(see also Atomic Age)

The world, says Wells,* is at the end of its tether. "The end of everything we call life is close at hand," he writes in his last literary statement, distributed by International News Service. We note, however, that Mr. Wells went to the trouble of taking out a world copyright on his world's end article. A prophet who was firmly convinced that the jig was up wouldn't feel any need of protecting his rights. We charge Mr. Wells with trying to play doom both ways.

— "Doomsday," November 17, 1945; *Writings from* The New Yorker, *1925–1976,* p. 229.

   * H. G. Wells, *Mind at the End of Its Tether* (London: Heinemann, 1945).

On Monday, man may be hysterical with doom, and on Tuesday you will find him opening the Doomsday Bar & Grill and settling down for another thousand years of terrifying queerness.

— "Doomsday," November 17, 1945; *Writings from* The New Yorker, *1925–1976,* p. 230.

Dreams
There is a period near the beginning of every man's life when he has little to cling to except his unmanageable dream, little to support him except good health, and nowhere to go but all over the place.

— "The Years of Wonder," March 13, 1961; *Points of My Compass,* p. 205, and *Essays of E. B. White,* p. 169.

When I think of how great a part of my life has been spent dreaming the hours away and how much of this total dream life has concerned small craft, I wonder about the state of my health, for I am told that it is not a good sign to be always voyaging into unreality, driven by imaginary breezes.

—"The Sea and the Wind That Blows," 1963; *Essays of E. B. White*, p. 205.

Sometimes, moving a broody as much as fifteen feet from her accustomed location will cause her to become unstuck, and she will take one look at the clutch of eggs and scream, "What's THAT?" Then she will take off into the sunset, scattering your dreams as she goes.

—Letter to Reginald Allen, March 5, 1973; *Letters of E. B. White*, Rev. Ed., pp. 591–592.

I have another terrier—a West Highland White, or Off White, named Susy. She is as open and outgiving as Jones is closed and reserved. Everybody loves Susy. Everybody tries to like Jones. But Jones takes his guard duties seriously and has made several attempts to kill people he thought were intruding. He particularly distrusts women in trousers, drivers of panel trucks, small children, and stray dogs....Sometimes I dream of owning another Norwich—one that looks like a Norwich and behaves like one. But I am known for my outsize dreams.

—Letter to Philip Hewes, March 20, 1974; *Letters of E. B. White*, Rev. Ed., p. 605.

My friend, John McNulty, had a title for a popular song he always intended to write and never did: "Keep your dreams within reason." We both thought this was a very funny idea for a song. I still think it is funny. My dreams have never been kept within reason. I'm glad they've not been.

—"The Art of the Essay, No. 1, E. B. White," interview with George A. Plimpton and Frank H. Crowther, Fall 1969; *Paris Review*, Issue 48.

Education
(see also College)

Our rich experiences, as a child, were secret, unexpected, and unreported. Sometimes they were vaguely obscene and calamitous; sometimes they were truancies of the mind during periods of extreme academic drowse. We are fairly sure that nothing in our face or in our manner ever gave us away during the onslaught of a rich experience. Adults can often tell when a child is gay, or troubled, or frightened, or amused; but a teacher who thinks she knows when a pupil is having a rich experience is just kidding herself.

— "Notes and Comment," February 8, 1936; *The New Yorker* and
  E. B. White: A Biography, by Scott Elledge, p. 21.

I have an increasing admiration for the teacher in the country school where we have a third-grade scholar in attendance. She not only undertakes to instruct her charges in all the subjects of the first three grades, but she manages to function quietly and effectively as a guardian of their health, their clothes, their habits, their mothers, and their snowball engagements. She has been performing this Augean task for twenty years and is both kind and wise. She cooks for the children on the stove that heats the room, and she can cool their passions or warm their soup with equal competence.

— "Education," March, 1939; *One Man's Meat*, p. 42.

I have always rather favored public school over private school, if only because in public school you meet a greater variety of children.

— "Education," March, 1939; *One Man's Meat*, p. 42.

The good world will be impossible to achieve until parents quit teaching their children about materialism....I teach my child* to look at life in a thoroughly materialistic fashion. If he escapes and becomes the sort of person I hope he will become, it will be because he sees through the hokum that I hand out. He already shows signs of it.

—"Sanitation," September, 1940; *One Man's Meat*, pp. 146–147.

* White's son Joel was nine, at the time.

Egg
(see also Birds, Chickens)

A bird setting on eggs is all eye and tail, a miracle of silent radiation and patience. It is almost impossible to meet, squarely, the accusing gaze of a broody bird, however unjust the accusation may seem. Perhaps this is because the bird's dedication is pure—untainted by the expectations of a hatch. (Nobody is more surprised than a hen bird when a shell opens and a chick comes out.)

—"Incubation," May 1, 1937; *Second Tree from the Corner*, p. 170.

Countries are ransacked, valleys drenched with blood. Though it seems untimely, I still publish my belief in the egg, the contents of the egg, the warm coal, and the necessity for pursuing whatever fire delights and sustains you.

—"Spring," April, 1941; *One Man's Meat*, p. 191.

The feeling I had as a boy for the miracle of incubation, my respect for the strange calm of broodiness, and my awe at an egg pipped from within after twenty-one days of meditation and prayer—these have diminished but slightly.

—"Introduction," *A Basic Chicken Guide for the Small Flock Owner*, by Roy E. Jones, p. viii.

I suspect there is a more plausible explanation for the popularity of the white egg in America. I ascribe the whole business to a busy little female—the White Leghorn hen. She is nervous, she is flighty, she is the greatest egg machine on two legs, and it just happens that she lays a white egg. She's never too distracted to do her job. A Leghorn hen, if she were on her way to a fire, would pause long enough to lay an egg.

—"Riposte," December, 1971; *Essays of E. B. White*, p. 61.

An unhatched egg is to me the greatest challenge in life.

—Letter to Reginald Allen, March 5, 1973; *Letters of E. B. White*, Rev. Ed., p. 592.

I don't know of anything in the world more wonderful to look at than a nest with eggs in it. An egg, because it contains life, is the most perfect thing there is. It is beautiful and mysterious.

—*Trumpet of the Swan* (spoken by Sam Beaver), 1970, p. 23.

The Egg has been an enduring theme in my life, and I have allowed my small flock of laying hens to grow old in service. Cosmetically they leave much to be desired, but their ovulation is brisk, and I greet them with the same old gag when I enter the pen: "White here. Cubism is dead."

—"Introduction," May 1982; *One Man's Meat*, p. xiii.

Elements of Style
(see Grammar, Language, Style)

Endorsements

If your public approval of a trademarked product and your influence can be bought at a price, then, carrying the thing through to an extreme, it is fair for General Motors to try to buy the good will of, say, the Secretary of State, and it is fair for the Secretary to consider selling it. He has a public trust as a servant of the state, you have a public trust as an avowed servant of the Muse or of History or whatever you want to call the thing that you and I do in the world. Our allegiance should be to our constituency, and we shouldn't grind axes as a sideline.

> —Letter to Alexander Woollcott, December 24, 1936; *Letters of E. B. White*, Rev. Ed., p. 139.

Whenever money changes hands, something goes along with it—an intangible something that varies with the circumstances.

> —"E. B. White Takes on Xerox and Wins," June 15, 1976; *New York Times* and *Letters of E. B. White*, Rev. Ed., p. 613.

Buying and selling space in news columns could become a serious disease of the press. If it reached epidemic proportions, it could destroy the press.

> —"E. B. White Takes on Xerox and Wins," June 15, 1976; *New York Times* and *Letters of E. B. White*, Rev. Ed., p. 614.

I don't want I.B.M. or the National Rifle Association providing me with a funded spectacular when I open my paper. I want to read what the editor and publisher have managed to dig up on their own—and paid for out of the till. . . .

> —"E. B. White Takes on Xerox and Wins," June 15, 1976; *New York Times* and *Letters of E. B. White*, Rev. Ed., p. 614.

English Usage
(see Grammar, Language, Style)

Entertainment

(see also Television)

We are really delighted about the Rockettes, who are at this moment on the high seas. Their pilgrimage is the finest thing that could happen to forty-six young ladies all at once. The Rockettes are hard-working, up early, up late, always drilling. Their precision is in the best West Point tradition and breathes the spirit of American uniformity. In our opinion, the Rockettes have a night in Paris coming to them. We love them, all forty-six torsos, all ninety-two legs. We don't know whether the girls are rehearsing on shipboard, but there is something about the idea of forty-six precision dancers kicking in a beam sea which appeals to us unreasonably.

— "Notes and Comment," June 26, 1937; *The New Yorker*, pp. 13–14.

My *Britannica* tells nothing about Mr. G. W. G. Ferris* but he belongs with the immortals.* From the top of the wheel, seated beside a small boy, windswept and fancy free, I looked down on the fair and for a moment was alive.

— "Security," September 1938; *One Man's Meat*, p. 11.

    * White's son Joel was 7 when this was written and this fair was probably the Blue Hill Fair, which continues today in Blue Hill, Maine. G. W. G. Ferris was the inventor of the Ferris Wheel.

It was encouraging to discover that there were still quite a few people at the fair who preferred a feeling of high, breezy insecurity to one of solid support.

— "Security," September 1938; *One Man's Meat*, p. 11.

The circus comes as close to being the world in microcosm as anything I know; in a way, it puts all the rest of show business in the shade. Its magic is universal and complex. Out of its wild disorder comes order; from its rank smell rises the good aroma of courage and daring; out of its preliminary shabbiness comes the final splendor.

    —"The Ring of Time," March 22, 1956; *Points of My Compass*, pp. 52–53, and *Essays of E. B. White*, p. 143.

For me the circus is at its best before it has been put together.... One ring is always bigger than three. One rider, one aerialist, is always greater than six. In short, a man has to catch the circus unawares to experience its full impact and share its gaudy dream.

    —"The Ring of Time," March 22, 1956; *Points of My Compass*, p. 53, and *Essays of E. B. White*, p. 143.

"The most fun there is," retorted Fern, "is when the Ferris wheel stops and Henry and I are in the top car and Henry makes the car swing and we can see everything for miles and miles."

    —*Charlotte's Web*, 1952, p. 173.

I would rather watch the circus or a ball game than ballet.

    —"The Art of the Essay, No. I, E. B. White," interview with George A. Plimpton and Frank H. Crowther, Fall 1969; *Paris Review*, Issue 48.

Equality

Woman...has slipped (or jumped) from the pedestal on which man had placed her. She has taken her seat alongside Man on the barstool and in the forum. She is doing, you might say, what comes naturally.

—"Introduction" (added in 1950), *Is Sex Necessary?*, by James Thurber and E. B. White, 2004 Ed., p. 9.

Faith
(see also Religion)

The matter of "faith" has been in the papers again lately. President Eisenhower...has come out for prayer and has emphasized that most Americans are motivated (as they surely are) by religious faith. The *Herald Tribune* headed the story, "PRESIDENT SAYS PRAYER IS PART OF DEMOCRACY." The implication in such a pronouncement, emanating from the seat of government, is that religious faith is a *condition,* or even a *precondition,* of the democratic life. This is just wrong.

—"A Letter from the East: Bedfellows," February 6, 1956; *Points of My Compass,* p. 44, and *Essays of E. B. White,* p. 85.

A President should pray whenever and wherever he feels like it (most Presidents have prayed long and hard, and some of them in desperation and agony), but I don't think a President should advertise prayer. That is a different thing.

—"A Letter from the East: Bedfellows," February 6, 1956; *Points of My Compass,* p. 44, and *Essays of E. B. White,* p. 85.

I hope that belief never is made to appear mandatory.

—"A Letter from the East: Bedfellows," February 6, 1956; *Points of My Compass,* p. 45, and *Essays of E. B. White,* p. 86.

I believe that our political leaders should live by faith and should, by deeds and sometimes by prayer, demonstrate faith, but I doubt that they should *advocate* faith, if only because such advocacy renders a few people uncomfortable. The concern of a democracy is that no honest man shall feel uncomfortable, I don't care who he is, or how nutty he is.

—"A Letter from the East: Bedfellows," February 6, 1956; *Points of My Compass*, p. 45, and *Essays of E. B. White*, p. 86.

Family
(see Fatherhood)

Farming
(see also Barn, Country Life, Gardening)

For all its implausibility, however, my farming has the excitement, the calamities, and sometimes the nobility of the real thing. For sheer surprise there is nothing to beat this life.

—"Clear Days," October 1938; *One Man's Meat*, p. 18.

I am farming, to a small degree and for my own amusement, but it is a cheap imitation of the real thing. I have fitted myself out with standard equipment, dungarees and a cap; but I would think twice before I dared stand still in a field of new corn. In the minds of my friends and neighbors who really know what they are about and whose clothes really fit them, much of my activity has the quality of a little girl playing house. My routine is that of a husbandman, but my demeanor is that of a high school boy in a soft-drink parlor.

—"Clear Days," October 1938; *One Man's Meat*, pp. 17–18.

For me, always looking for an excuse to put off work, a farm is the perfect answer, good for twenty-four hours of the day. I find it extremely difficult to combine manual labor with intellectual, so I compromise and just do the manual. Since coming to the country I have devoted myself increasingly to the immediate structural and surgical problems that present themselves to any farmer, be he ever so comical in his methods and his designs. I have drifted farther and farther from my muse, closer and closer to my post-hole digger.

—"The Practical Farmer," August 1940; *One Man's Meat*, pp. 140–141.

Farming is about twenty per cent agriculture and eighty per cent mending something that has got busted. Farming is a sort of glorified repair job.

—"The Practical Farmer," August 1940; *One Man's Meat*, p. 143.

A good farmer is nothing more nor less than a handy man with a sense of humus.

—"The Practical Farmer," August 1940; *One Man's Meat*, p. 143.

Last fall I hauled rockweed up from the shore and spread it to a depth of five or six inches on the dirt floor of the sheep shed and covered it with straw. Now the sheep droppings are accumulating on this rockweed base and forming a rich dressing for the land. There is no doubt about it, the basic satisfaction in farming is manure, which always suggests that life can be cyclic and chemically perfect and aromatic and continuous.

—"A Winter Diary," January 1941; *One Man's Meat*, p. 171.

I keep telling myself that it is time to quit this place, with its eleven rooms and its forty acres, and cut myself down to size. I may still do it. But I can envision what would happen if I did: I would no sooner get comfortably settled in a small house on an acre of land than I would issue instructions to build a small barn and attach it to the house through a woodshed. A bale of hay would appear mysteriously in the barn, and there would soon be a bantam rooster out there, living in the style to which he feels he should be accustomed. I would be right back where I started.

—"Introduction," May 1982; *One Man's Meat,* pp. xiii–xiv.

Fatherhood
(see also Future, Time)

The time not to become a father is eighteen years before a world war.
—"Answers to Hard Questions," March 11, 1939; *The New Yorker.*

But when I got back there, with my boy, and we settled into a camp near a farmhouse and into the kind of summertime I had known, I could tell that it was going to be pretty much the same as it had been before—I knew it, lying in bed the first morning, smelling the bedroom and hearing the boy sneak quietly out and go off along the shore, in a boat. I began to sustain the illusion that he was I, and therefore, by simple transposition, that I was my father. This sensation persisted, kept cropping up all the time we were there. It was not an entirely new feeling, but in this setting it grew much stronger. I seemed to be living a dual existence. I would be in the middle of some simple act, I would be picking up a bait box or laying down a table fork, or I would be saying something, and suddenly it would be not I but my father who was saying the words or making the gesture. It gave me a creepy sensation.

—"Once More to the Lake," August 1941; *Essays of E. B. White,*
p. 198.

Found my wife and son and dachshund, all three, sitting under a lap robe on the back porch in the beautiful sunlight this afternoon listening to the Cornell-Yale game on a portable radio, this being the first time in two weeks my boy had been out of bed and the first time the dog had attended a Cornell game. (He was shaking like a leaf with pent-up emotion, and Cornell was behind.) But the three of them looked very wonderful and comical sitting there in their private bowl, and I laughed out loud.

> —"A Week in November," November 1942; *One Man's Meat,*
> p. 268.

Fear

How contagious hysteria and fear are! In my henhouse are two or three jumpy hens, who, at the slightest disturbance, incite the whole flock to sudden panic—to the great injury, nervously and sometimes physically, of the group. This panic is transmitted with great rapidity; in fact, it is almost instantaneous, like the wheeling of pigeons in air, which seem all to turn and swoop together as though controlled electrically by a remote fancier.

> —"Hot Weather," July 1939, *One Man's Meat,* p. 72.

I am bothered chiefly by my little fears that are the same as they were almost 70 years ago. I was born scared and am still scared. This has sometimes tested my courage almost beyond endurance.

> —"E. B. White: Notes and Comment by Author," interview with
> Israel Shenker, July 11, 1969; *New York Times.*

My panic fear, as near as I can make out, is not of death. It is an amorphous fear, lacking in form.
—Letter to Scott Elledge, May 25, 1982; *Letters of E. B. White*, Rev. Ed., p. 649.

Freedom
(see also Freedom of Speech)

An hour of freedom is worth a barrel of slops.
—*Charlotte's Web* (spoken by the goose to Wilbur the pig), 1952, p. 23.

Safety is all well and good: I prefer freedom.
—*Trumpet of the Swan* (Louis the swan to the zookeeper), 1970, p. 170.

I resent the patronizing air of persons who find in my plain belief in freedom a sign of immaturity. If it is boyish to believe that a human being should live free, then I'll gladly arrest my development and let the rest of the world grow up.
—"Freedom," July 1940; *One Man's Meat*, p. 135.

To be free, in a planetary sense, is to feel that you belong to earth. To be free, in a social sense, is to feel at home in a democratic framework.
—"Freedom," July 1940; *One Man's Meat*, p. 138.

There is a lot of the cat in me, and cats are not joiners.
—"Compost," June 1940, *One Man's Meat*, p. 129.

Freedom has great moral strength; this is its principal advantage over Communism. Freedom has the strength of the spirit. Freedom is strong economically—in the United States and in many other capitalist countries. It is strong in military power. But it is sadly lacking in political strength, because it does not enjoy the benefits of political unity and, unlike Communism, does not lay the course for it. Two free nations, though they may pull together in a crisis, are almost as far apart diplomatically as a free nation and a Communist nation.

—"Letter from the East,"* June 18, 1960; *The New Yorker.*

> * This article (on the subject of disarmament) in its entirety was entered into the Congressional Record by the Hon. Frank E. Moss of Utah on June 29, 1960.

Freedom of Speech
(see also Freedom)

"What do you paint when you paint on a wall?"
  Said John D.'s grandson Nelson.
"Do you paint just anything at all?
"Will there be any doves, or a tree in fall?
"Or a hunting scene, like an English hall?"

"I paint what I see," said Rivera.

—"I Paint What I See"* (excerpt), May 20, 1933; *The New Yorker,* reprinted in *Poems and Sketches of E. B. White,* 1981, p. 35.

> * Subtitled "A Ballad of Artistic Integrity on the Occasion of the Removal of Some Rather Expensive Murals from the RCA Building in the Year 1933." John D's grandson was Nelson Rockefeller, who evidently considered the painting too Bolshevik.

In time of war, the State cuts deeply into the citizen's right to know. The State sits in the editor's chair and draws the editor's mantle close. A piece of fiction by a soldier came into this office the other day, and it had obviously been censored not only for reasons of security but for reasons of taste. The Army censor had not liked the way one of the characters talked, so he had removed some of the conversation. We get goose pimples when we feel the blue pencil being taken gently out of our hands. We wish to remind censors that it is a very old pencil. Somebody gave it to us in 1791, and we wouldn't lose it for anything.

—*The Wild Flag*, February 3, 1945, p. 58.

I am a member of a party of one, and I live in an age of fear. Nothing lately has unsettled my party and raised my fears so much as your editorial, on Thanksgiving Day, suggesting that employees should be required to state their beliefs in order to hold their jobs. The idea is inconsistent with our constitutional theory and has been stubbornly opposed by watchful men since the early days of the Republic. I can only assume that your editorial writer, in a hurry to get home for Thanksgiving, tripped over the First Amendment and thought it was the office cat.*

—Letter to the *New York Herald Tribune*, November 29, 1947; *Letters of E. B. White*, Rev. Ed., p. 267.

* Published by the *New York Herald Tribune* December 2, 1947, after the *Tribune* had supported the right of the movie industry to blacklist the "Hollywood Ten" and any others who refused to answer questions before the House Un-American Activities Committee.

There are always plenty of people who are ready to stifle opinion they don't admire, and if the opinion happens to be expressed in a volume of sound that is in itself insufferable, the number of people who will want to stifle both the sound *and* the fury will greatly increase.

—"Sound," June 19, 1948; *Second Tree from the Corner,* p. 114, and *Notes on Our Times,* p. 42.

I have yet to see a piece of writing, political or non-political, that does not have a slant. All writing slants the way a writer leans, and no man is born perpendicular, although many men are born upright. The beauty of the American free press is that the slants and the twists and the distortions come from so many directions, and the special interests are so numerous, and the reader must sift and sort and check and countercheck in order to find out what the score is. This he does. It is only when a press gets its twist from a single source, as in the case of government controlled press systems, that the reader is licked.

—"Talk of the Town," February 18, 1956; *The New Yorker.*

Under the press, I presume the Fund will examine the tendency of newspapers to die or merge, leaving a city like Bangor, Maine, without an opposition press.* Under television I should think the Fund might notice the fact that performers of all kinds (newscasters, actors, singers, entertainers, commentators) have been persuaded to speak the commercial. The sound of news and the sound of soap are a blur in the ear—an unhealthy condition essentially, I think.... There is nothing much to be "taught" about equality—you either believe it or you don't. But there is much that can be taught about rights and about liberty, including the basic stuff: that a right derives from a responsibleness, and that men become free as they become willing to accept restrictions on their acts.

—Letter to Robert M. Hutchins, January 4, 1957; *Letters of E. B. White,* Rev. Ed., p. 394.

* Hutchins, president of the Fund for the Republic, had asked

White to comment on a prospectus setting forth the Fund's program on civil liberties.

Friendship

Many of my friends are the writers of books, and I find it ruffling to hunt around book titles for a balance (sometimes extremely delicate) between delight and friendship.

    —Letter to Irita Van Doren, November 13, 1951; *Letters of E. B. White*, Rev. Ed., p. 315.

        * Once a year, Mrs. Van Doren, editor of the *New York Herald Tribune* literary supplement, wrote to a list of well-known people, asking each to name the three books he or she had enjoyed most in the past year. White asked to be taken off her list of readers.

When you took leave of Ross* after a calm or stormy meeting, he always ended with the phrase that has become as much a part of the office as the paint on the walls. He would wave his limp hand, gesturing you away. "All right," he would say. "God bless you." Considering Ross's temperament and habits, this was a rather odd expression. He usually took God's name in vain if he took it at all. But when he sent you away with this benediction, which he uttered briskly and affectionately, and in which he and God seemed all scrambled together, it carried a warmth and sincerity that never failed to carry over. The words are so familiar to his helpers and friends here that they provide the only possible way to conclude this hasty notice and to take our leave.

    —*The New Yorker*, December 15, 1951.

        * Obituary for founder and editor of *The New Yorker*, Harold Ross.

"Why did you do all this for me?" he asked. "I don't deserve it. I've never done anything for you."

"You have been my friend," replied Charlotte. "That in itself is a tremendous thing."
—*Charlotte's Web*, 1952, p. 164.

I wove my webs for you because I liked you. After all, what's a life, anyway? We're born, we live a little while, we die. A spider's life can't help being something of a mess, with all this trapping and eating flies. By helping you, perhaps I was trying to lift up my life a trifle. Heaven knows anyone's life can stand a little of that.
—*Charlotte's Web*, 1952, p. 164.

It is not often that someone comes along who is a true friend and a good writer.
—*Charlotte's Web*, 1952, p. 184.

Future
(see also Fatherhood, Time)

The future, wave or no wave, seems to me no unified dream but a mince pie, long in the baking, never quite done.
—Review of Anne Morrow Lindbergh's *The Wave of the Future*, December, 1940; *One Man's Meat*, pp. 165–166.

Gardening
(see also Farming)

Plant shallow
   Right side up

In a pot
Not a cup.
Let the earth not be fallow.

Keep dark
Two weeks
Till the germ
Speaks
Water four times and remark.

Bring to light,
Water daily,
Greet the flower
Gaily,
See that all is done right.

—"Lines for an Amaryllis Keeper (Bulb under Separate Cover),"
January 11, 1930; *The New Yorker.*

The movers experience the worst trouble with two large house plants,
six-footers, in their great jars. The jars, on being sounded, prove to be a
third full of water and have to be emptied into the gutter. Living things
are always harder to lift, somehow, than inanimate objects, and I think
any mover would rather walk up three flights with a heavy bureau than
go into a waltz with a rubber plant. There is really no way for a man
to put his arms around a big house plant and still remain a gentleman.

—"Sootfall and Fallout," October 18, 1956; *Points of My Compass,*
p. 78, and *Essays of E. B. White,* p. 91.

One afternoon, I found my wife kneeling at the edge of her peren-
nial border on the north side, trying to disengage Achillea-the-Pearl
from Coral Bell. "If I could afford it," she said bitterly, "I would take
every damn bit of Achillea out of this border." She is a woman in

comfortable circumstances, arrived at through her own hard labor, and this sudden burst of poverty, and her inability to indulge herself in a horticultural purge, startled me. I was so moved by her plight and her unhappiness that I went to the barn and returned with an edger, and we spent a fine, peaceable hour in the pretty twilight, rapping Achillea over the knuckles and saving Coral Bell.

—"A Report in Spring," 1957; *Points of My Compass*, p. 114, and *Essays of E. B. White*, p. 16.

Government
(see also Democracy)

Sometimes we wonder if our government is not just an expensive hobby of a people accustomed to spend money. It is appalling how much time and substance a citizen gives to his own governing. The income-tax report, longer and harder than an anagram; the quarterly payments which must be remembered; the melancholy hours with lawyers, expert accountants, and other technicians; the long trips to the internal revenue corridors of the Fisk Building, bringing "all your books;" the serving on juries; the getting off serving on juries; the licensing of dogs; the licensing of automobiles; tedious afternoons with blank forms of one kind or another, which always demand detailed information about forgotten relatives.

—"Notes and Comment," February 23, 1929; *The New Yorker.*

It* has been called crackpot, but that doesn't disparage it for me. Genius is more often found in a cracked pot than in a whole one. In the main I prefer to be experimented on by an idealist than allowed to lie fallow through a long dry reactionary season.

—"Lime," November 1940; *One Man's Meat*, p. 158.

* The administration of Franklin D. Roosevelt.

Government is the thing. Law is the thing. Not brotherhood, not international co-operation, not security councils that can stop war only by waging it. Where do human rights arise, anyway? In the sun, in the moon, in the daily paper, in the conscientious heart? They arise in responsible government. Where does security lie, anyway—security against the thief, the murderer, the footpad? In brotherly love? Not at all. It lies in government.

> —*The Wild Flag,* June 1, 1946, p. 187, reprinted in *Common Cause: A Monthly Report of the Committee to Frame a World Constitution,* vol. I, no. 2, August, 1947.

Grammar
(see also Language, Style)

[A] schoolchild should be taught grammar—for the same reason that a medical student should study anatomy. Having learned about the exciting mysteries of an English sentence, the child can then go forth and speak and write any damn way he pleases.

> —"The Living Language," February 23, 1957; *Writings from* The New Yorker, *1925–1976,* p. 142.

The next grammar book I bring out I want to tell how to end a sentence with five prepositions. A father of a little boy goes upstairs after supper to read to his son, but he brings the wrong book. The boy says, "What did you bring that book that I don't want to be read to out of up for?"

> —Letter to J. G. Case, March 30, 1962; *Letters of E. B. White,* Rev. Ed., p. 447.

I had a letter in today's mail that began, "Dear Friend: We have had serious computer problems with our mailing list which has just been resolved." It's clear that this man faces a problem far more grievous than a balky computer and knows not where his real problem lies. What this world needs, Tony, is a good five-cent school teacher.

—Letter to D. Anthony English, ca. September 16, 1983; *Letters of E. B. White*, Rev. Ed., p. 668.

Gratitude

Geese are great to have around, because they stir the air. They are sagacious, contentious, storm-loving, and beautiful. They are natural hecklers, delight in arguing a point, and are possessed of a truly remarkable sense of ingratitude. They never fail to greet you on your arrival, and the greeting is tinged with distaste and sarcasm.

—Letter to Mason Trowbridge, November 18, 1972; *Letters of E. B. White*, Rev. Ed., p. 589.

When days, by ending make me old;
When neither fortune comes nor gold,
When love, with eyes that speak the truth,
Backs slowly from me, like my youth,
And friends who know their way alone
Go forth and leave me, one by one;
Still must I very thankful be
For things that are a part of me.
That when I read a pretty line
A little flame goes down my spine,
That when I see the morning sun
I laugh to think the world's begun.

—"*For Things That Are a Part of Me*" (in its entirety from "The Conning Tower"), July 13, 1926.*

* This was the verse that prompted Katharine S. Angell, the *New Yorker* editor who later would become White's wife, to write

on July 15, 1926 and ask him to "drop in at the office to discuss various thoughts we have in mind for you in connection with *The New Yorker.*"—White Literary LLC archive.

Health

These are the antibiotic days, when even newborn pigs are removed to sanitary surroundings, to be raised on laboratory milk, innocent of any connection with the sow.

    —"Remembrance of Things Past," *Second Tree from the Corner,* pp. 125–126, and *Notes on Our Times,* p. 89.

My doctor has ordered me to put my head in traction for ten minutes twice a day. (Nobody can figure out what to do with my head, so now they are going to give it a good pull, like an exasperated mechanic who hauls off and gives his problem a smart jolt with the hammer.) I have rigged a delightful traction center in the barn, using a canvas halter, a length of clothesline, two galvanized pulleys, a twelve-pound boat anchor, a milking stool, and a barn swallow. I set everything up so I could work the swallow into the deal, because I knew he would enjoy it, and he does. While his bride sits on the eggs and I sit on the milking stool, he sits on a harness peg a few feet away, giggling at me throughout the ten-minute period and giving his mate a play-by-play account of man's fantastic battle with himself, which in my case must look like suicide by hanging.

    —"Coon Tree," June 14, 1956; *Points of My Compass,* pp. 61–62, and *Essays of E. B. White,* p. 34.

Incidentally, I was pleased to learn, not long ago, that children in unsanitary homes acquire a better resistance to certain diseases (polio and hepatitis among them) than children in homes where sanitation is king.

—"Coon Tree," June 14, 1956; *Points of My Compass*, p. 75, and *Essays of E. B. White*, p. 45.

Don't worry about my health—I am a lot better and plenty good enough for my purposes. I had two things the matter with me—mice in the subconscious and spurs in the cervical spine. Of the two the spine trouble was less bothersome. It took me eighteen months to find out how you get rid of mice.... Anyway, here I am, in the clear again and damned thankful to be there. I can work without falling apart, and can sleep—which is quite refreshing after a year and a half.

—Letter to Stanley Hart White, January, 1945; *Letters of E. B. White*, Rev. Ed., p. 249.

My family doctor, circa 1906, had a simple, direct approach to hay fever. He told my father to spray my head with cold water before breakfast every morning, and my father did. I rather miss it.

—Unpublished letter to Dr. Ralph Bowen, February 2, 1954; The E. B. White Collection, Carl A. Kroch Library, Cornell University, Ithaca, NY.

I've always felt that my hypochondria was greatly exaggerated.... I don't regret the time I spent worrying about myself. Things do happen to people, and only a very unimaginative, lumpish sort of person could go through life without conjuring up a few personal disasters. I knew a girl once who pricked her finger on a Victrola needle and although it was a tiny scratch, it developed into a first-class infection that had to be taken very seriously by the doctors. If I tend to pour a few drops of peroxide on a surface wound, it isn't because I am a violent hypochondriac, it's because I have a strong sense of disaster, rooted in solid experience.

—Letter to Judith Preusser, March 19, 1984; *Letters of E. B. White,* Rev. Ed., p. 679.

Home
(see also House)

Home is the place where the queer things are:
Hope and compassion and objets d'art.

—"Home Song" (excerpt), February 5, 1944; *The New Yorker.*

Home is the strangest of common places,
Drenched with the light of familiar faces.

—"Home Song" (excerpt), February 5, 1944; *The New Yorker.*

Home is the proving ground of sanity,
Brick and ember, love and vanity.

—"Home Song" (excerpt), February 5, 1944; *The New Yorker.*

Home is the part of our life that's arable,
Home is a pledge, a plan, a parable.

—"Home Song" (excerpt), February 5, 1944; *The New Yorker.*

Ever before us is home's immensity,
Always within us its sheer intensity.

—"Home Song" (excerpt), February 5, 1944; *The New Yorker.*

It is not possible to keep abreast of the normal tides of acquisition. A home is like a reservoir equipped with a check valve: the valve permits influx but prevents outflow.

—"Good-Bye to 48th Street," November 12, 1957; *Points of My Compass*, p. 126, and *Essays of E. B. White*, p. 4.

If it happens to be an auxiliary cruising boat, it is without question the most compact and ingenious arrangement for living ever devised by the restless mind of man—a home that is stable without being stationary, shaped less like a box than like a fish or a bird or a girl, and in which the homeowner can remove his daily affairs as far from shore as he has the nerve to take them, close-hauled or running free—parlor, bedroom, and bath, suspended and alive.

—"The Sea and the Wind That Blows," 1963; *Essays of E. B. White*, p. 205.

Dear Mr. President:
Thank you for your friendly greetings on my 70th birthday. I was very pleased to have them.

I'm afraid your letter crossed a brisk telegram from my wife to you demanding that you call off the moon shot. But that's the way life is in this household: something coming in, something going out, all with the best of all possible motives if not with the most sophisticated coordination.

—Letter to President Richard M. Nixon, July 15, 1969; *Letters of E. B. White*, Rev. Ed., p. 529.

Hope

Only hope can carry us aloft, can keep us afloat. Only hope, and a certain faith that the incredible structure that has been fashioned by this most strange and ingenious of all the mammals cannot end in ruin and disaster. This faith is a writer's faith, for writing itself is an act of faith, nothing else. And it must be the writer, above all others, who keeps it alive—choked with laughter, or with pain.

    —Speech in acceptance of the *National Medal for Literature,* 1971; *E. B. White: A Biography,* by Scott Elledge, p. 348.

As long as there is one upright man, as long as there is one compassionate woman, the contagion may spread and the scene is not desolate. Hope is the thing that is left to us, in a bad time. I shall get up Sunday morning and wind the clock, as a contribution to order and steadfastness.

    —Letter to Mr. Nadeau, March 30, 1973; *Letters of E. B. White,* Rev. Ed., p. 596.

It is quite obvious that the human race has made a queer mess of life on this planet. But as a people we probably harbor seeds of goodness that have lain for a long time, waiting to sprout when the conditions are right. Man's curiosity, his relentlessness, his inventiveness, his ingenuity have led him into deep trouble. We can only hope that these same traits will enable him to claw his way out.

    —Letter to Mr. Nadeau, March 30, 1973; *Letters of E. B. White,* Rev. Ed., p. 596.

Hang onto your hat. Hang onto your hope. And wind the clock, for tomorrow is another day.

    —Letter to Mr. Nadeau, March 30, 1973; *Letters of E. B. White,* Rev. Ed., p. 596.

House
(see also Home)

Our advice to anyone* suddenly possessed of an old farmhouse is to hire a fox terrier to remodel it, and wait ten years before allowing a contractor on the premises.
—"Notes and Comment," December 5, 1953; *The New Yorker.*
* This piece began: "One of the things Ike and Mamie [Eisenhower] are doing these days is remodelling an old farmhouse in Pennsylvania."

One solution [the American Society of Industrial Designers] offered for the house of the future is to have a place called a "dirty room." This would be equipped with appliances for all cleaning problems, and into it would be dumped everything dirty. But in most American homes the way to have a dirty room is to have a small boy; that's the way *we* worked it for a number of happy years.
—"Coon Tree," June 14, 1956; *Points of My Compass,* p. 70, and *Essays of E. B. White,* p. 41.

Our kitchen today is a rich, intoxicating blend of past, present, and future; basically it belongs to the past when it was conceived and constructed. It is a strange and implausible room, dodolike to the modern eye but dear to ours, and far from dead. In fact, it teems with life of all sorts—cookery, husbandry, horticulture, canning, planning. It is an arsenal, a greenhouse, a surgical-dressing station, a doghouse, a bathhouse, a lounge, a library, a bakery, a cold-storage plant, a factory, and a bar, all rolled up into one gorgeous ball, or ballup. In it you can find the shotgun and shell for shooting up the whole place if it ever should become obsolete; in it you can find the molasses cookie if you ever decide just to sit down and leave everything the way it is.

—"Coon Tree," June 14, 1956; *Points of My Compass*, pp. 70–71, and *Essays of E. B. White*, p. 41.

Our kitchen contains such modern gadgets as an electric refrigerator, a Macy cabinet, and a Little Dazey ice smasher, and it contains such holdovers from the past as the iron stove, the roller towel, the iron sink, the wooden drainboard, and the set tubs. (You can wash a dog in my kitchen without any trouble except from the dog.)

—"Coon Tree," June 14, 1956; *Points of My Compass*, p. 71, and *Essays of E. B. White*, pp. 41–42.

My house has a living room that is at the core of everything that goes on: it is a passageway to the cellar, to the kitchen, to the closet where the phone lives. There's a lot of traffic. But it's a bright, cheerful room, and I often use it as a room to write in, despite the carnival that is going on all around me.

—"The Art of the Essay, No. I, E. B. White," interview with George A. Plimpton and Frank H. Crowther, Fall 1969; *Paris Review*, Issue 48.

Humor

One of the things commonly said about humorists is that they are really very sad people—clowns with a breaking heart....But there is often a rather fine line between laughing and crying, and if a humorous piece of writing brings a person to the point where his emotional responses are untrustworthy and seem likely to break over into the opposite realm, it is because humor, like poetry, has an extra content.

It plays close to the big hot fire which is Truth, and sometimes the reader feels the heat.

——"Some Remarks on Humor,"* 1941; *Essays of E. B. White*, pp. 243–244.

* Adapted from *A Subtreasury of American Humor*, 1941, co-authored by Katharine S. White and E. B. White.

The world likes humor, but it treats it patronizingly. It decorates its serious artists with laurel, and its wags with Brussels sprouts. It feels that if a thing is funny it can be presumed to be something less than great, because if it were truly great it would be wholly serious. Writers know this, and those who take their literary selves with great seriousness are at considerable pains never to associate their name with anything funny or flippant or nonsensical or "light." They suspect it would hurt their reputation, and they are right.

——"Some Remarks on Humor," adapted from *A Subtreasury of American Humor*, 1941; *Essays of E. B. White*, p. 244.

Humor can be dissected, as a frog can, but the thing dies in the process and the innards are discouraging to any but the pure scientific mind.

——"Some Remarks on Humor," adapted from *A Subtreasury of American Humor*, 1941; *Essays of E. B. White*, p. 243.

Whatever else an American believes or disbelieves about himself, he is absolutely sure he has a sense of humor.

——"Some Remarks on Humor," adapted from *A Subtreasury of American Humor*, 1941; *Essays of E. B. White*, p. 245.

I don't think I agree that humor must preach in order to live; it need only speak the truth——and I notice it usually does.

——"Some Remarks on Humor," adapted from *A Subtreasury of American Humor*, 1941; *Essays of E. B. White*, p. 249.

Hypochondria
(see Health)

Junk Mail

Part of our duty shall always be to suggest ways of defeating the United States mails and lessening the menace of business correspondence. We have recently worked out a remarkably effective new counter-offensive for the persons who send reply envelopes, either stamped or unstamped, with their advertising circulars. Let us say that you receive an offer of twelve tins of beef extract for a dollar thirty-nine. In the same mail you probably also receive the special discount offer of a publisher of a book on marriage. Merely place the beef-extract reply card in the publisher's return envelope, and vice versa, and mail them. That takes care of everybody.
—"Notes and Comment," June 8, 1929; *The New Yorker.*

I haven't gotten round to installing a mail chute into my furnace, but I'm working on a plan to make it illegal for mail order houses to buy and sell mailing lists—which is where the trouble really starts. I would like to go to court and testify that it is an invasion of my privacy to reveal my whereabouts in return for money.
—Letter to Mr. Bemis, February 1, 1981; *Letters of E. B. White,* Rev. Ed., p. 638.

Justice

I think that the most precious thing in the world is not the concept of federation but the concept of justice—that is, justice as it has been developed in the western world. The only sort of One-World that I would settle for, is a One-World firmly based on that type of justice.

—Letter to Janice White, April 27, 1952; *Letters of E. B. White*, Rev. Ed., pp. 327–328.

The Supreme Court said nothing about silliness, but I suspect it may play more of a role than one might suppose. People are, if anything, more touchy about being thought silly than they are about being thought unjust.

—"The Ring of Time," March 22, 1956; *Points of My Compass*, p. 58, and *Essays of E. B. White*, p. 147.

I doubt whether justice, which is the forerunner of peace, will ever be pulled out of a hat, as some suppose. Justice will find a home where there is a synthesis of liberty and unity in a framework of government. And when justice appears on any scene, on any level of society, men's problems enjoy a sort of automatic solution, because they enjoy the means of solution. Unity is no mirage. It is the distant shore. I believe we should at least head for that good shore, though most of us will not reach it in this life.

—"Letter from the East,"* June 18, 1960; *The New Yorker*.

* This article (on the subject of disarmament) in its entirety was entered into the Congressional Record by the Hon. Frank E. Moss of Utah on June 29, 1960.

Kennedy, John F.

It can be said of him, as of few men in a like position, that he did not fear the weather, and did not trim his sails, but instead challenged the wind itself, to improve its direction and to cause it to blow more softly and more kindly over the world and its people.

—"John F. Kennedy," *The New Yorker* obituary, November 30, 1963, reprinted in *Writings from* The New Yorker, *1925–1976,* p. 235.

As they walked out of the Presidential office, Mr. Kennedy took a white handkerchief from his pocket and wiped the boy's nose.—The *Times*

A President's work is never done,
His burdens press from sun to sun:
A Berlin wall, a racial brew,
A tax-cut bill, a Madame Nhu.
One crisis ebbs, another flows—
        And here comes John with a runny nose.

A President must rise and dress,
See senators, and meet the press,
Be always bold, be sometimes wary,
Be kind to foreign dignitary,
And while he's fending off our foes
        Bend down and wipe a little boy's nose.

—"Burdens of High Office," October 12, 1963; *The New Yorker.*

When we think of him, he is without a hat, standing in the wind and weather. He was impatient of topcoats and hats, preferring to be exposed, and he was young enough and tough enough to confront and to enjoy the cold and the wind of these times, whether the winds of nature or the winds of political circumstance and national danger. He died of exposure, but in a way that he would have settled for—in the line of duty, and with his friends and enemies all around, supporting him and shooting at him.

—"John F. Kennedy," *The New Yorker* obituary, November 30, 1963, reprinted in *Writings from* The New Yorker, *1925–1976,* p. 235.

Landscape

In the loveliest town of all, where the houses were white and high
and the elm trees were green and higher than the houses, where the
front yards were wide and pleasant and the back yards were bushy and
worth finding out about, where the streets sloped down to the stream
and the stream flowed quietly under the bridge, where the lawns ended
in orchards and the orchards ended in fields and the fields ended in
pastures and the pastures climbed the hill and disappeared over the
top toward the wonderful wide sky, in this loveliest of all towns,
Stuart stopped to get a drink of sarsaparilla.
—*Stuart Little*, 1945, p. 100.

"There's something about north," he said, "something that sets it
apart from all other directions. A person who is heading north is not
making any mistake, in my opinion."

"That's the way I look at it," said Stuart. "I rather expect that from
now on I shall be traveling north until the end of my days."

"Worse things than that could happen to a person," said the
repairman.

"Yes, I know," answered Stuart.
—*Stuart Little*, 1945, p. 129.

"Following a broken telephone line north, I have come upon some
wonderful places," continued the repairman. "Swamps where cedars
grow and turtles wait on logs but not for anything in particular;
fields bordered by crooked fences broken by years of standing still;
orchards so old they have forgotten where the farmhouse is. In the
north I have eaten my lunch in pastures rank with ferns and junipers,
all under fair skies with a wind blowing. My business has taken me
into spruce woods on winter nights where the snow lay deep and soft,

a perfect place for a carnival of rabbits. I have sat at peace on the freight platforms of railroad junctions in the north, in the warm hours and with the warm smells. I know fresh lakes in the north, undisturbed except by fish and hawk and, of course, by the Telephone Company, which has to follow its nose. I know all these places well. They are a long way from here—don't forget that. And a person who is looking for something doesn't travel very fast."

—*Stuart Little*, 1945, pp. 129–131.

My own vision of the land—my own discovery of its size and meaning—was shaped, more than by any other instrument, by a Model T Ford. The vision endures; the small black roadster is always there, alive and kicking, a bedroll wedged against its spare, a dictionary sprawling on its floor, an Army trunk bracketed to its left running board. The course of my life was changed by it, and it is in a class by itself. It was cheap enough so I could afford to buy one; it was capable enough so it gave me courage to start.

—*Farewell to Model T; From Sea to Shining Sea*, p. 34.

As for bringing the view into line, the front of our dwelling is within a hundred and eighty degrees of a magnificent view, and the only really sensible thing we did twenty years ago when we acquired it was to let the view worry along on its own. This it has done. The way you get to the view at our place is to walk through the kitchen, then through the woodshed to the barn, then through the barn to a small, cobwebby window in the rear, and there it is. That's where it belongs, too. Nothing can be more paralyzing than living in constant touch with a view. A view is like a bottle of champagne: it should be held in reserve in the cellar, not piped into the living room, where everyone is at its mercy morning, noon, and night.

—"Notes and Comment," December 5, 1953; *The New Yorker*.

It was the Narramissic that once received as fine a lyrical tribute as was ever paid to a river—a line in a poem by a schoolboy, who wrote of it, "It flows though Orland [Maine] every day." I never cross that mild stream without thinking of the testimonial to the constancy, the dependability of small, familiar rivers.

—"Homecoming," December 10, 1955; *Points of My Compass*, p. 30, and *Essays of E. B. White*, p. 9.

Language
(see also Grammar, Style)

Usage seems to us peculiarly a matter of ear. Everyone has his own prejudices, his own set of rules, his own list of horribles.

—"English Usage," January 30, 1937; *Second Tree from the Corner*, p. 150.

The English language is always sticking a foot out to trip a man.

—"English Usage," January 30, 1937; *Second Tree from the Corner*, p. 151.

English usage is sometimes more than mere taste, judgment, and education—sometimes it's sheer luck, like getting across a street.

—"English Usage," January 30, 1937; *Second Tree from the Corner*, p. 151.

Write with nouns and verbs, not with adjectives and adverbs. The adjective hasn't been built that can pull a weak or inaccurate noun out of a tight place.

—"An Approach to Style," *The Elements of Style*, 1959; 2nd Ed., 1972, p. 64.

Avoid fancy words. Avoid the elaborate, the pretentious, the coy and the cute. Do not be tempted by a twenty-dollar word when there is a ten-center handy, ready and able.

—"An Approach to Style," *The Elements of Style*, 1959; 2nd Ed., 1972, p. 69.

Leisure

We ran across the phrase "leisure class" the other day and it stopped us cold, so quaint did it sound, so fragrant with the spice of yesteryear. You used to read a good deal about the leisure class, but something seems to have happened to it. One thing that may have happened to it is that too many people joined it and the point went out of it.

—"Leisure Class," August 8, 1953; *Writings from* The New Yorker, *1925–1976*, p. 219.

If your refrigerator quits making ice cubes on a Saturday afternoon (as ours did recently) or if you lose a gall bladder on Times Square after the Saturday-evening show, you might just as well walk over to the river, tie a rock to your foot, and jump in. Your repairman and your doctor are in the Catskills, probably fishing from the same boat.

—"Leisure Class," August 8, 1953; *Writings from* The New Yorker, *1925–1976*, p. 220.

Leisure used to have a direct relationship to wealth, but even that seems to have changed. A lot of people who are independently wealthy cannot properly claim to belong to the leisure class anymore: they are too nerved up to be leisurely and too heavily taxed to be completely relieved of the vulgar burden of finding a livelihood.

—"Leisure Class," August 8, 1953; *Writings from* The New Yorker, *1925–1976*, p. 219.

Letters

The visitor to the attic knows the risk he runs when he lifts the lid from a box of old letters. Words out of the past have the power to detain. Hours later he may find himself still crouched on the floor, savoring the pains and embarrassments of an early love, and with leg cramps to boot.
—"Foreword," July 30, 1932; *Points of My Compass*, p. xi.

It never occurred to me, when I got into this thing, that it was an entirely different kind of exposure from the ones I had been used to as a writer of prose pieces. A man who publishes his letters becomes a nudist—nothing shields him from the world's gaze except his bare skin. A writer, writing away, can always fix things up to make himself more presentable, but a man who has written a letter is stuck with it for all time.
—*Letters of E. B. White*, ed. Dorothy Lobrano Guth, 1st edition, 1976, back cover.

Liberty
(see Freedom)

Life

At eight of a hot morning, the cicada speaks his first piece. He says of the world: heat. At eleven of the same day, still singing, he has not changed his note but has enlarged his theme. He says of the morning: love. In the sultry middle of the afternoon, when the sadness of love and of heat has shaken him, his sympathetic soul goes into the great movement and he says: death. But the thing isn't over. After supper he weaves heat, love, death into a final stanza, subtler and less brassy than the others. He has one last heroic monosyllable at his command. Life, he says, reminiscing. Life.

—"Life," September 1, 1945; *Writings from* The New Yorker, *1925–1976*, p. 3.

After all, what's a life, anyway? We're born, we live a little while, we die.

—*Charlotte's Web*, 1952, p. 164.

A statement you must have? 'Tis your own choosing.

Let's see.... Well, how is this? *Life is amusing.*

—"On Being Asked for a Statement" (poem excerpt, final two lines); *Poems and Sketches of E. B. White*, 1981, p. 108.

There is no one to sit on [the goose eggs] but me, and I had to return to New York, so I ordered a trio of Muscovies from a man in New Hampshire, in the hope of persuading a Muscovy duck to give me a Toulouse gosling. (The theme of my life is complexity-through-joy.)

—"A Report in Spring," May 10, 1957; *Points of My Compass*, p. 113, and *Essays of E. B. White*, p. 16.

I have no faith, only a suitcaseful of beliefs that sustain me. Life's meaning has always eluded me and I guess always will. But I love it just the same.

—Letter to Mary Virginia Parrish, August 29, 1969; *Letters of E. B. White*, Rev. Ed., p. 532.

To celebrate life properly, it is of great advantage to gain the confidence and the attention of a child, for children are the great celebrants.

—Acceptance speech for the George G. Stone Center for Children's Books, ca. 1970; The E. B. White Collection, Carl A. Kroch Library, Cornell University, Ithaca, NY.

Literature
(see also Poets and Poetry, Writing and Writers)

To us literature is still a thing of letters; we are old-fashioned enough to believe that great writing, like ours, should be read, not listened to perhaps inattentively. We believe in the sanctity of type, in the beauty of the muted page, in the discipline required in the following with the eye the well-punctuated, yet always imperfect expression of a writer's thought.
—"Talk of the Town," July 13, 1935; *The New Yorker.*

I don't know which is more discouraging, literature or chickens.
—Letter to James Thurber, November 18,1938; *Letters of E. B. White,* Rev. Ed., p. 177.

In a free country it is the duty of writers to pay no attention to duty. Only under a dictatorship is literature expected to exhibit an harmonious design or an inspirational tone.
—"Salt Water Farm," January, 1939; *One Man's Meat,* p. 34.

Love

The word "love" is loosely used by writers, and they know it. Furthermore, the word "love" is accepted loosely by readers, and *they* know it. There are many kinds of love but for the purposes of this article I shall confine my discussion to the usual hazy interpretation: the strange bewilderment that overtakes one person on account of another person. Thus, when I say love in this article, you will take it to mean *the pleasant confusion which we know exists.* When I say passion, I *mean* passion.
—*Is Sex Necessary?,* by James Thurber and E. B. White, 2004 Ed., p. 54.

Animal love is the marvelous force
Marsupials take it as a matter of course;
You find it in Aryan, Mongol, Norse,
In beetle, tarantula, ostrich, horse;
It creeps in the grasses and blows in the gorse,
It's something all sponges were bound to indorse—
And only in humans it causes remorse.

> —Last stanza of "Lines Long after Santayana" (subtitle: Animal
> Love Is a Marvelous Force.—"The Life of Reason"), February
> 3, 1934; *The New Yorker*, p. 21.

We must not fall into the error of the committee that recently elected
the "prettiest schoolteacher in the United States" and published her
name and photograph. The prettiest schoolteacher in the United
States is, we submit, a woman who runs into the tens of millions; she
is the one locked in the heart of every scholar, young or old, who was
ever in love with his teacher.

> —"Notes and Comment," January 3, 1953; *The New Yorker.*

Loyalty

It is easier for a man to be loyal to his club than to his planet; the bylaws
are shorter, and he is personally acquainted with the other members.

> —"Intimations," December, 1941; *One Man's Meat*, p. 222.

As it turns out, a very great majority of Americans are deeply worried, not because they have a skeleton in their closet or because they
disapprove of fact-finding in Congress,* but because they see and feel
in their daily lives the subtle changes that has already been worked by
a runaway loyalty-checking system in the hands of a few men who, to

say it in a whisper, are not ideally equipped to handle the most delicate and dangerous job in the nation, that is the questioning of values of one's fellow citizens. A couple of these committeemen don't know a fact from a bag of popcorn anyway.

—"Note and Comment," March 7, 1953; *The New Yorker.*

 * Senator Joseph McCarthy had become chairman of the Senate Permanent Subcommittee on Investigations in 1953.

Luck

My numbers were lucky ones: July is the seventh month, and I appeared on the eleventh day. Seven, eleven. I've been lucky ever since and have always counted heavily on luck.

—"Mount Vernon," 1976; *Letters of E. B. White,* Rev. Ed, p. 7.

The terrible urge of the multitudes to participate in the chancy side of life, to recover the gift they were cheated out of by their lack of capital and their lack of initiative, is everywhere discernible. It accounts for the enormous preoccupation with pinball games, numbers games, bingo, race horses, stock markets, pools, lotteries—millions of people called "common" trying to make up for the fact that their normal activities still bring them only a flat and unchangeable payment in a world that is neither flat nor unchangeable. Even in a last extremity, with neither money nor hope, a man seizes a deck of cards and tries to win at solitaire, to restore himself and taste the wine of luck.

—"Control," December 1942; *One Man's Meat,* p. 273.

Luck is not something you can mention in the presence of the self-made man.

—"Control," December 1942; *One Man's Meat,* p. 273.

As Louis relaxed and prepared for sleep, all his thoughts were of how lucky he was to inhabit such a beautiful earth, how lucky he had been to solve his problems with music, and how pleasant it was to look forward to another night of sleep and another day tomorrow, and the fresh morning, and the light that returns with the day.

—*Trumpet of the Swan*, 1970, p. 210.

My two bantam hens are both sitting, but all during the days when they were laying their clutch of eggs, I had to visit the barn every night and bring the eggs indoors so they wouldn't freeze, then return them to the nests in the morning so the hens wouldn't think they had been robbed. This wouldn't have been such an onerous chore if bantams ever chose an accessible place for nesting, but you should see where these two birds of mine decided to set up housekeeping. Only a small, wiry, determined old man in his dotage could reach the nests on hands and knees, so high and so remote are they. A bantam hen isn't happy unless she is in a high, remote place, impossible to get to by any normal person. I was lucky to be born abnormal. It ran in the family.

—Letter to Mrs. Dorothy Guth, ca. March 16, 1984; *Letters of E. B. White*, Rev. Ed., p. 678.

Maine
(see also Country Life)

The pollen count has been high, and my hay fever has raged quietly all through the customary membranes. It's suicide for me to arrive here on July first, but I do it anyway. I would really rather feel bad in Maine than good anywhere else.

—Letter to Charles G. Muller, July 11, 1937; *Letters of E. B. White*, Rev. Ed, p. 149.

What happens to me when I cross the Piscataqua and plunge rapidly into Maine at a cost of seventy-five cents in tolls? I cannot describe it. I do not ordinarily spy a partridge in a pear tree, or three French hens, but I do have the sensation of having received a gift from a true love.

— "Home-Coming," *Points of My Compass*, p. 30, and *Essays of E. B. White*, December 10, 1955, p. 9.

You can certainly learn to spell "moccasin" while driving into Maine, and there is often little else to do, except steer and avoid death.

— "Home-Coming," *Points of My Compass*, p. 29, and *Essays of E. B. White*, December 10, 1955, p. 8.

Yet, sometime in the winter of 1938, or even before that, I became restless. I felt unhappy and cooped up. More and more my thoughts turned to Maine, where we owned a house with a barn attached. I don't recall being disenchanted with New York—I loved New York. I was certainly not disenchanted with *The New Yorker*—I loved the magazine. If I was disenchanted at all, I was probably disenchanted with *me*.

— "Introduction," May 1982; *One Man's Meat*, p. xii.

Once in everyone's life there is apt to be a period when he is fully awake, instead of half asleep. I think of those first five years in Maine as the time when this happened to me. . . . I was suddenly seeing, feeling, and listening as a child sees, feels, and listens. It was one of those rare interludes that can never be repeated, a time of enchantment. I am fortunate indeed to have had the chance to get some of it down on paper.

— "Foreword," May 1982; *One Man's Meat*, p. xiii.

Maine Speech

For the word "all" you use the phrase "the whole of." You ask, Is that the whole of it?" And whole is pronounced hull. Is that the hull of it? It sounds as though you might mean a ship.
—"Maine Speech," October 1940; *One Man's Meat,* p. 154.

For lift, the word is heft. You heft a thing to see how much it weighs.
—"Maine Speech," October 1940; *One Man's Meat,* p. 154.

When you are holding a wedge for somebody to tap with a hammer, you say: "Tunk it a little." I've never heard the word tap used. It's always tunk.
—"Maine Speech," October 1940; *One Man's Meat,* p. 154.

Baster (pronounced bayster) is a popular word with boys. All the kids use it. He's an old baster, they say, when they pull an eel out of an eel trap. It probably derives from bastard, but it sounds quite proper and innocent when you hear it, and rather descriptive. I regard lots of things now (and some people) as old basters.
—"Maine Speech," October 1940; *One Man's Meat,* p. 154.

A person who is sensitive to cold is spleeny. We have never put a heater in our car, for fear we might get spleeny.
—"Maine Speech," October 1940; *One Man's Meat,* p. 154.

A windy day is a "rough" day, whether you are on land or sea. Mild weather is "soft." And there is a distinction between weather overhead and weather underfoot. Lots of times, in spring, when the ground is muddy, you will have a "nice day overhead."
—"Maine Speech," October 1940; *One Man's Meat,* p. 155.

When a sow has little ones, she "pigs." Mine pigged on a Sunday, the ol' baster.
—"Maine Speech," October 1940; *One Man's Meat*, p. 156.

The final "y" of a word becomes "ay." Our boy used to call our dog Freddie. Now he calls him Fredday. Sometimes he calls him Fredday dee-ah; other times he calls him Fredday you ol' baster.
—"Maine Speech," October 1940; *One Man's Meat*, p. 156.

Marriage

Our hasty opinion is that what is happening to marriage is this—every husband is in the attic writing an article called "What is Happening to Marriage?" and every wife is at her desk in the editorial office of a magazine dictating notes to authors saying: "Dear Mr. Zerphus, It occurs to us that we could use a little article of thirty-five hundred words on the subject 'What is Happening to Marriage?' Wouldn't you like to write it?"
—"Notes and Comment," March 23, 1929; *The New Yorker*.

It was a very nice wedding—nobody threw anything, and there was a dog fight.*
—"The Most Beautiful Decision," *Letters of E. B. White*, Rev. Ed., p. 81.
   * White was describing his marriage to Katharine Sergeant Angell in November, 1929.

What Pope Pius* seemed to us to have missed completely about Christian marriage was this: that, with all its falling from grace, it is still a lot of fun; more fun than practically any other form of institutionalized living, more fun than a picnic, so much fun, in fact, that almost everyone still believes in it pretty thoroughly, even the most violent reformers and renovators. Rome never said a word about that, and missed a big chance.

 —"Notes and Comment," January 17, 1931; *The New Yorker.*

  * In a published encyclical about marriage, birth control, and divorce titled *Casti Connubli* (i.e., of chaste wedlock).

We were talking about marriage, the institution that still runs up and down Madison Avenue like an old Ford, and which some people still hang on to, as they might to an old Ford that gives trouble. As for righteous living, we doubt if marriage abets it. To live righteously…a man probably ought to stay celibate. Celibacy is a cinch as compared with wedlock.

 —"Notes and Comment," April 25, 1931; *The New Yorker.*

We've just received a letter from a man in Appleton, Wisconsin, enclosing three newsbreaks (those little items we print at the bottom of the page) for our consideration. His letter ends, "I hope one or more of these sees print in *The New Yorker,* for I am becoming weary of hearing my wife describe *her* newsbreak acceptances as 'my published works.'" There, obviously, is a marriage headed for the rocks.

 —"Notes and Comment," October 11, 1969; *The New Yorker.*

Middle Age
(see Aging)

Miracles

"I don't know why you say a web is a miracle—it's just a web."
"Ever try to spin one?" asked Dr. Dorian.

 —*Charlotte's Web* (Fern's mother, then Dr. Dorian), 1952, p. 109.

We had a good crop this year (enough to feed ten families), but we use cow manure, not Miracle-Gro. A cow is something of a miracle herself, and it seems to get passed along to the tomatoes.

—Letter to Evelyn M. Hickey, October 16, 1980; *Letters of E. B. White*, Rev. Ed., p. 637.

There is always the miracle of the by-products. Plane a board, the shavings accumulate around your toes ready to be chucked into the stove to kindle your fire (to warm your toes so you can plane a board). Draw some milk from a creature to relieve her fullness, the milk goes to a little pig to relieve his emptiness. Drain some oil from a crankcase, and you smear it on the roosts to control the mites. The worm fattens on the apple, the young goose fattens on the wormy fruit, the man fattens on the young goose, the worm awaits the man.

—"Cold Weather," March 1943; *One Man's Meat*, p. 275.

Moon

The moon, it turns out, is a great place for men. One-sixth gravity must be a lot of fun, and when Armstrong and Aldrin* went into their bouncy little dance, like two happy children, it was a moment not only of triumph but of gaiety. The moon, on the other hand, is a poor place for flags. Ours looked stiff and awkward, trying to float on the breeze that does not blow.

—"Moon Landing," July 26, 1969; *Writings from* The New Yorker, *1925–1976*, p. 102.

* Of the Apollo II mission, July 20, 1969.

Like every great river and every great sea, the moon belongs to none and belongs to all.

—"Moon Landing," July 26, 1969; *Writings from* The New Yorker, *1925–1976*, p. 102.

Morning

If the world were merely seductive, that would be easy. If it were merely challenging, that would be no problem. But I arise in the morning torn between a desire to improve (or save) the world and a desire to enjoy (or savor) the world. This makes it hard to plan the day.

—"E. B. White: Notes and Comment by Author," interview with Israel Shenker, July 11, 1969; *New York Times*; quoted in *E. B. White: A Biography*, by Scott Elledge, p. 300.

Stuart was an early riser: he was almost always the first person up in the morning. He liked the feeling of being the first one stirring; he enjoyed the quiet rooms with the books standing still on the shelves, the pale light coming in through the windows, and the fresh smell of day.

—*Stuart Little*, 1945, p. 13.

Nationalism
(see also Atomic Age, Peace)

It is easier to plan a good world than a good nation, or even a good hemisphere. Nothing can be worked out to the advantage of the human race as long as the mind is hampered and cramped by existing boundaries, however unfortified.

—"Compost," June 1940; *One Man's Meat*, pp. 130–131.

Who is there big enough to love the whole planet? We must find such people for the next society.*

—"Intimations," December 1941; *One Man's Meat*, p. 222.

* Originally written three days after Pearl Harbor was attacked.

Nationalism has two fatal charms for its devotes: it presupposes local self-sufficiency, which is a pleasant and desirable condition, and it suggests, very subtly, a certain personal superiority by reason of one's belonging to a place that is definable and familiar, as against a place that is strange, remote.

　　—"Intimations," December 1941; *One Man's Meat,* p. 222.

Clubs, fraternities, nations—these are the beloved barriers in the way of a workable world, these will have to surrender some of their rights and some of their ribs. A "fraternity" is the antithesis of *fraternity.* The first (that is, the order or organization) is predicated on the idea of exclusion; the second (that is, the abstract thing) is based on a feeling of total equality....Fraternity begins when the exclusion formula is found to be distasteful.

　　—"One Man's Meat" column, February 1942; *Harper's.*

A nation asks of its citizens everything—their fealty, their money, their faith, their time, their lives. It is fair to ask whether the nation, in return, does indeed any longer serve the best interests of the human beings who give so lavishly of their affections and their blood.

　　—"Preface," 1946; *The Wild Flag,* p. x.

Whether we wish it or not, we may soon have to make a clear choice between the special nation to which we pledge our allegiance and the broad humanity of which we are born a part. This choice is implicit in the world to come. We have a little time in which we can make the choice intelligently. Failing that, the choice will be made for us in the confusion of war, from which the world will emerge unified—the unity of total desolation.

　　—"Preface," 1946; *The Wild Flag,* pp. x–xi.

To speak as though we've got law when what we've got is treaties and pacts, to use the word "law" for non-law, is to lessen our chances of ever getting law among nations, since the first step toward getting it is to realize, with dazzling clearness, that we haven't got it and never have had it.

—"Notes and Comment," May 8, 1943; *The New Yorker.*

The thing we find hard to understand about supremacy is why, if it is right for America, it isn't right for every other nation.

—*The Wild Flag,* August 12, 1944, p. 32.

Everybody likes to hear about a man laying down his life for his country, but nobody wants to hear about a country giving her shirt for her planet. Why is that? You would think that after such a demonstration of self-sacrifice as we have seen, any nation would gladly bleed and die for the world. Who are we to play the peace safe?

—*The Wild Flag,* September 9, 1944, p. 35.

Remember, an intelligence service is, in fact, a stupidity service; if we were really intelligent, we wouldn't be willing to stake our children's lives on our country's spies.

—*The Wild Flag,* March 2, 1946, p. 159.

Every country is entitled to a few mistakes. The Vietnam war is a mistake. The Selective Service is inequitable. Yet even a country that is in the midst of a mistake must have an armed force loyal to its basic beliefs and prepared to defend its general principles. If that were to go, all would go.

—"E. B. White: Notes and Comment by Author," interview with Israel Shenker, July 11, 1969; *New York Times.*

Nature

The spider, dropping down from twig,
Unwinds a thread of his devising:
A thin, premeditated rig
To use in rising.
And all the journey down through space,
In cool descent, and loyal-hearted,
He builds a ladder to the place
From which he started.

Thus I, gone forth, as spiders do,
In spider's web a truth discerning,
Attach one silken strand to you
For my returning.

> —"Natural History," written for Katharine S. White,* November
> 30, 1929; *Letters of E. B. White*, Rev. Ed., pp. 88–89.
>> * E. B. and Katharine White had been married on November
>> 13, 1929.

In the kitchen cabinet is a bag of oranges for morning juice. Each orange is stamped "Color Added." The dyeing of an orange, to make it orange, is man's most impudent gesture to date. It is really an appalling piece of effrontery, carrying the clear implication that Nature doesn't know what she is up to.

> —"On a Florida Key," February 1941; *Essays of E. B. White*, p. 139.

I guess I remembered clearest of all the early mornings, when the lake was cool and motionless, remembered how the bedroom smelled of the lumber it was made of and of the wet woods whose scent entered through the screen. The partitions in the camp were thin and did not extend clear to the top of the rooms, and as I was always the first up I would dress softly so as not to wake the others, and sneak out into the sweet outdoors and start out in the canoe, keeping close along the shore in the long shadows of the pines. I remembered being very careful never to rub my paddle against the gunwale for fear of disturbing the stillness of the cathedral.

   —"Once More to the Lake," August 1941; *Essays of E. B. White*, p. 198.

Before you can be an supranationalist you have to first be a naturalist and feel the ground under you making a whole circle.

   —"Intimations," December 1941; *One Man's Meat*, p. 222.

If the vexatious world of people were the whole world, I would not enjoy it at all. But it is only a small, though noisy, part of the whole; and I find the natural world as engaging and as innocent as it ever was. When I get sick of what men do, I have only to walk a few steps in another direction to see what spiders do. Or what the weather does. This sustains me very well indeed and I have no complaints.

   —Letter to Carrie A. Wilson, May 1, 1951; *Letters of E. B. White*, Rev. Ed., p. 306.

I don't know whether a passionate love of the natural world can be transmitted or not, but like the love of beauty it is a thing one likes to associate with the scheme of inheritance.

   —Letter to Stanley Hart White, March 11, 1954; *Letters of E. B. White*, Rev. Ed., p. 356.

   * To his brother, in reference to the 100th anniversary of their father's birth.

I would feel more optimistic about a bright future for man if he spent less time proving that he can outwit Nature and more time tasting her sweetness and respecting her seniority.

——"Coon Tree," June 14, 1956; *Points of My Compass,* p. 67, and *Essays of E. B. White,* p. 39.

I think man's gradual, creeping contamination of the planet, his sending up of dust into the air, his strontium additive to our bones, his discharge of industrial poisons into rivers that once flowed clear, his mixing of chemicals with fog on the east wind add up to a fantasy of such grotesque proportions as to make everything said on the subject seem pale and anemic by contrast. I hold one share in the corporate earth and am uneasy about the management.... The correct amount of strontium with which to impregnate the topsoil is *no* strontium.... I belong to a small, unconventional school that believes that *no* rat poison is the correct amount to spread in the kitchen where children and puppies can get at it. I believe that *no* chemical waste is the correct amount to discharge into the fresh rivers of the world, and I believe that if there is a way to trap the fumes from factory chimneys, it should be against the law to set these deadly fumes adrift where they can mingle with the fog and given the right conditions, suddenly turn an aura into another Donora, Pa.

——"Sootfall and Fallout," October 18, 1956; *Points of My Compass,* pp. 80–81, and *Essays of E. B. White,* pp. 92–93.

"Welcome to the pond and the swamp adjacent!" he said. "Welcome to the world that contains this lonely pond, this splendid marsh, unspoiled and wild! Welcome to sunlight and shadow, wind and weather; welcome to water! The water is a swan's particular element, as you will soon discover. Swimming is no problem for a swan."

——*Trumpet of the Swan* (the old cob to his newborn cygnets), 1970, pp. 30–31.

Newspapers

People believe almost anything they see in print.
  —*Charlotte's Web*, 1952, p. 89.

The first duty of a newspaper is to stay alive.
  —"Death of the *Sun*," January 14, 1950; *Second Tree From the Corner*,
  p. 163.

The most important single fact about any newspaper is that it differs from the next newspaper and is owned by a different man, or group of men. This fact (the fact of difference) transcends a newspaper's greatness, a newspaper's honesty, a newspaper's liveliness, or any other quality. The health of the country deteriorates every time a newspaper dies of strangulation or is wiped out in a mercy killing.
  —"Death of the *Sun*," January 14, 1950; *Second Tree from the Corner*,
  p. 163.

I was a flop as a daily reporter. Every piece had to be a masterpiece—and before you knew it, Tuesday was Wednesday.
  —"E. B. White: Notes and Comment by Author," interview with
  Israel Shenker, July 11, 1969; *New York Times*.

The press in our free country is reliable and useful not because of its good character but because of its great diversity. As long as there are many owners, each pursuing his own brand of truth, we the people have the opportunity to arrive at the truth and to dwell in the light. The multiplicity of ownership is crucial. It's only when there are few owners, or, as in a government-controlled press, one owner, that the truth becomes elusive and the light fails. For a citizen in our free society, it is an enormous privilege and a wonderful protection to have access to hundreds of periodicals, each peddling its own belief. There is safety in numbers: the papers expose each other's follies and peccadilloes, correct each other's mistakes, and cancel out each other's biases. The reader is free to range around in the whole editorial bouillabaisse and explore it for the one clam that matters—the truth.

—Letter to W. B. Jones, January 30, 1976; *Letters of E. B. White*, Rev. Ed., p. 613.

New York City
(see also City Life, Country Life)

Its Strengths
New York is the concentrate of art and commerce and sport and religion and entertainment and finance, bringing to a single compact arena the gladiator, the evangelist, the promoter, the actor, the trader and the merchant.

—*Here Is New York*, 1949, p. 19.

The City of New York is a world government on a small scale. There, truly, is the world in a nutshell, its citizens meeting in the subway and ballpark, sunning on the benches in the square. They shove each other, but seldom too hard. They annoy each other, but rarely to the point of real trouble.

—"Preface," 1946; *The Wild Flag*, pp. xii–xiii.

On any person who desires such queer prizes, New York will bestow the gift of loneliness and the gift of privacy....No one should come to New York to live unless he is willing to be lucky.

—*Here Is New York*, 1949, p. 19.

There are roughly three New Yorks. There is, first, the New York of the man or woman who was born here, who takes the city for granted and accepts its size and its turbulence as natural and inevitable. Second, there is the New York of the commuter—the city that is devoured by locust each day and spat out each night. Third, there is the New York of the person born somewhere else and came to New York in quest of something.

—*Here Is New York*, 1949, pp. 25–26.

Commuters give the city its tidal restlessness; natives give it solidity and continuity; but the settlers give it passion.

—*Here Is New York*, 1949, pp. 25–26.

A poem compresses much in a small space and adds music, thus heightening its meaning. The city is like poetry: it compresses all life, all races and breeds, into a small island and adds music and the accompaniment of internal engines. The island of Manhattan is without any doubt the greatest human concentrate on earth, the poem whose magic is comprehensible to millions of permanent residents but whose full meaning will always remain elusive.

—*Here Is New York*, 1949, p. 29.

It* is to the nation what the white church spire is to the village—the visible symbol of aspiration and faith, the white plume saying that the way is up.

—*Here Is New York*, 1949, p. 31.

    * Manhattan.

New York provides not only a continuing excitation but also a spectacle that is continuing.

—*Here Is New York*, 1949, p. 38.

The two moments when New York seems most desirable, when the splendor falls all round about and the city looks like a girl with leaves in her hair, are just as you are leaving and must say goodbye, and just as you return and can say hello.

—"New York," June 11, 1955; *Writings from* The New Yorker, *1925–1976*, p. 207.

Its Vulnerabilities

The city, for the first time in its long history, is destructible. A single flight of planes no bigger than a wedge of geese can quickly end this island fantasy, burn the towers, crumble the bridges, turn the underground passages into lethal chambers, cremate the millions. The intimation of mortality is part of New York now: in the sound of jets overhead, in the black headlines of the latest edition.

—*Here Is New York*, 1949, p. 54.

All dwellers in cities must live with the stubborn fact of annihilation; in New York the fact is somewhat more concentrated because of the concentration of the city itself, and because, of all targets, New York has a certain clear priority. In the mind of whatever perverted dreamer might loose the lightning, New York must hold a steady, irresistible charm.

—*Here Is New York*, 1949, p. 54.

The city at last perfectly illustrates both the universal dilemma and the general solution, this riddle in steel and stone is at once the perfect target and the perfect demonstration of nonviolence, of racial brotherhood, this lofty target scraping the skies and meeting the destroying planes halfway, home of all people and all nations, capital of everything, housing the deliberations by which the planes are to be stayed and their errand forestalled.

—*Here Is New York*, 1949, p. 56.

In New York, a citizen is likely to keep on the move, shopping for the perfect arrangement of rooms and vistas, changing his habitation according to fortune, whim, and need. And in every place he abandons he leaves something vital, it seems to me, and starts his new life somewhat less encrusted, like a lobster that has shed its skin and is for a time soft and vulnerable.

——"Good-Bye to 48th Street," November 12, 1957; *Points of My Compass,* p. 129, and *Essays of E. B. White,* p. 6.

Someone could suggest that since Manhattan is a small island, unexpendable, it poses a limit to building and to population. Nobody ever suggests this—it would be heresy to suggest it. Yet most of the ills of New York are attributable to a too great concentration in too small a space. Every time you look up, somebody has erected another tall office building or another tall apartment building. Homes are disappearing. Traffic grinds to a halt. New York is an inspiring city, a fantastic city, but I think it is crowding its luck. Structural steel can be its undoing. Without homes, a city loses its quality. It is no longer a city, it is just a happening.

——"E. B. White: Notes and Comment by Author," interview with Israel Shenker, July 11, 1969; *New York Times.*

It is a miracle that New York works at all. The whole thing is implausible. Every time the residents brush their teeth, millions of gallons of water must be drawn from the Catskills and the hills of Westchester.

——*Here Is New York,* 1949, p. 31.

The New Yorker (magazine)
(see also Ross, Harold and Thurber, James)

Commas in *The New Yorker* fall with the precision of knives in a circus act, outlining the victim.

— "The Art of the Essay, No. I, E. B. White," interview with George A. Plimpton and Frank H. Crowther, Fall 1969; *Paris Review*, Issue 48.

We write as we please, and the magazine publishes as *it* pleases. When the two pleasures coincide, something gets into print. When they don't, the reader draws a blank. It is a system we recommend—the only one, in fact, under which we are willing to be kept.

— "Editorial Writers," March 4, 1944; *Writings from* The New Yorker, *1925–1976*, pp. 27–28.

Of course, a good deal depends on the aims of a publication. The more devious the motives of his employer, the more difficult for a writer to write as he pleases. As far as we have been able to discover, the keepers of this house have two aims: the first is to make money, the second is to make sense. We have watched for other motives, but we have never turned up any. That makes for good working conditions, and we write this as a sort of small, delayed tribute to our house.

— "Editorial Writers," March 4, 1944; *Writings from* The New Yorker, *1925–1976*, p. 28.

Nothing

"What do you mean *less* than nothing?" replied Wilbur. "I don't think there is any such thing as *less* than nothing. Nothing is absolutely the limit of nothingness. It's the lowest you can go. It's the end of the line. How can something be less than nothing? If there were something that

was less than nothing, then nothing would not be nothing, it would be something—even though it's just a very little bit of something. But if nothing is *nothing*, then nothing has nothing that is less than *it* is."
—*Charlotte's Web*, 1952, p. 28.

Passion

Understanding the principles of passion is like knowing how to drive a car; once mastered, all is smoothed out; no more does one experience the feeling of perilous adventure, the misgivings, the diverting little hesitancies, the wrong turns, the false starts, the glorious insecurity. All is smoothed out, and all, so to speak, is lost.
—*Is Sex Necessary?*, by James Thurber and E. B. White, 2004 Ed., p. 53.

Peace
(see also Atomic Age, Nationalism, War)

We will never get anywhere till we stop talking about "all peace-loving nations." The phrase is "all nations."
—*The Wild Flag*, September 9, 1944, p. 36.

Peace is expensive, and so are human rights and civil liberties; they have a price, and we the peoples have not yet offered to pay it. Instead we are trying to furnish our globe with these precious ornaments the cheap way, holding our sovereignty cautiously in one fist while extending the other hand in a gesture of co-operation. In the long run this will prove the hard way, the violent way. The United Nations

Organization, which in its present form is a league of disunited nations whose problems are on the tables and whose spies are behind the arras, is our last chance to substitute order for disorder, government for anarchy, knowledge for espionage. We better make it good.
— *The Wild Flag*, March 2, 1946, pp. 158–159.

Most people think of peace as a state of Nothing Bad Happening, or Nothing Much Happening. Yet if peace is to overtake us and make us the gift of serenity and well-being, it will have to be the state of Something Good Happening. What is this good thing? I think it is the evolution of community, community slowly and surely invested with the robes of government by the consent of the governed. We cannot conceivably achieve a peaceful life merely by relaxing the tensions of sovereign nations; there is an unending supply of them.
— "Unity," June 4, 1960; *Points of My Compass*, p. 178, and *Essays of E. B. White*, p. 101.

Photography

Photography is the most self-conscious of the arts. The act of photography has been glorified in the news picture magazine, and even in the newspapers. Publisher and reader enjoy shoptalk together. The editor continually points to "best shots," or "news picture of the week," confident that his clientele is following every move of the shutter.
— "Peaks in Journalism," July 24, 1937; *Second Tree from the Corner*, p. 158. [See also *In the Words of E. B. White*, p. 212]

And the package contained school photographs, which we eagerly studied. Our youngest grandson had done something odd with his mouth, in a manly attempt to defeat the photographer, and looked just like Jimmy Hoffa. "How marvelous!" said my wife.

—"What Do Our Hearts Treasure?" January 1966; *Essays of E. B. White*, p. 153.

Poets and Poetry
(see also Literature, Writing and Writers)

I sound as though I were contemptuous of poets; the fact is I am jealous of them. I would rather be one than anything.

—"Poetry," November 1939; *One Man's Meat*, p. 95.

Poetry Defined

To me, poetry is what is memorable, and a poet is a fellow or girl who lets drops a line that get remembered in the morning.

—"Preface," *Poems and Sketches of E. B. White*, 1981, p. xiv.

I think poetry is the greatest of the arts. It combines music and painting and story-telling and prophecy and the dance. It is religious in tone, scientific in attitude. A true poem contains the seed of wonder; but a bad poem, egg-fashion, stinks.

—"Poetry," November 1939; *One Man's Meat*, pp. 93–94.

I think there is no such thing as a long poem. If it is long it isn't a poem; it is something else. A book like *John Brown's Body*, for instance, is not a poem—it is a series of poems tied together with cord. Poetry is intensity, and nothing is intense for long.

—"Poetry," November 1939; *One Man's Meat*, p. 94.

A poem compresses much in a tight space and adds music, thus heightening its meaning.
—*Here Is New York*, 1949, p. 29.

Poets Defined

Broadly speaking, a major poet may be told from a minor poet in two ways: (1) by the character of the verse, (2) by the character of the poet. (Note: it is not always advisable to go into the character of the poet.)
— "How to Tell a Major Poet from a Minor Poet," November 8, 1930; *The New Yorker*, reprinted in *Quo Vadimus? or, the Case for the Bicycle*, 1938, p. 69.

All poets who, when reading from their own works, experience a choked feeling, are major. For that matter, all poets who read from their own works are major, whether they choke or not.
— "How to Tell a Major Poet from a Minor Poet," November 8, 1930; *The New Yorker*, reprinted in *Quo Vadimus? or, the Case for the Bicycle*, 1938, p. 72.

All women poets, dead or alive, who smoke cigars are major.
— "How to Tell a Major Poet from a Minor Poet," November 8, 1930; *The New Yorker*, reprinted in *Quo Vadimus? or, the Case for the Bicycle*, 1938, p. 72.

All poets named Edna St. Vincent Millay are major.
— "How to Tell a Major Poet from a Minor Poet," November 8, 1930; *The New Yorker*, reprinted in *Quo Vadimus? or, the Case for the Bicycle*, 1938, p. 73.

A poet who, in a room full of people, is noticeably keeping at a little distance and "seeing into" things is a major poet.

—"How to Tell a Major Poet from a Minor Poet," November 8, 1930; *The New Yorker*, reprinted in *Quo Vadimus? or, the Case for the Bicycle*, 1938, p. 74.

Obscurity vs. Clarity

A poet dares be just so clear and no clearer; he approaches lucid ground warily, like a mariner who is determined not to scrape his bottom on anything solid. A poet's pleasure is withholding a little of his meaning, to intensify by mystification. He unzips the veil from beauty but does not remove it. A poet utterly clear is a trifle glaring.

—"Poetry," November 1939; *One Man's Meat*, p. 93.

There are many types of poetical obscurity. There is the obscurity that results from the poet's being mad. This is rare. Madness in poets is as uncommon as madness in dogs.

—"Poetry," November 1939; *One Man's Meat*, p. 94.

A discouraging number of reputable poets are sane beyond recall. There is also the obscurity that is the result of the poet's wishing to appear mad, even if only a little mad. This is rather common and rather dreadful. I know of nothing more distasteful than the work of a poet who has taken leave of his reason deliberately, as a commuter might of his wife.

—"Poetry," November 1939; *One Man's Meat*, p. 94.

The Process

Diligence in a poet is the same as dishonesty in a bookkeeper. There are rafts of bards who are writing too much, too diligently, and too slyly. Few poets are willing to wait out their pregnancy—they prefer to have a premature baby and allow it to incubate after being safely laid in casino Old Style.

—"Poetry," November 1939; *One Man's Meat,* p. 95.

Inner thought: it is easier to make rhymes on a train; the lines come out the right length because the wheel clicks never miss their count. Idea: if we were a poet we would spend all our time on trains.

—"The Talk of the Town," January 2, 1932; *The New Yorker.*

When it comes to poetry I take my own sweet time and allow myself no more than one poem a day. A good poem is like an anchovy: it makes you want another right away and pretty soon the tin is empty and you have a bellyache or a small bone in your throat or both.

—Letter to Philip Booth,* November 22, 1970; *Letters of E. B. White,* Rev. Ed., p. 558.

   * Philip Booth had sent White a copy of his poetry collection *Margins.*

Polls

The so-called science of poll-taking is not a science at all but mere necromancy. People are unpredictable by nature, and although you can take a nation's pulse, you can't be sure that the nation hasn't just run up a flight of stairs, and although you can take a nation's blood pressure, you can't be sure that if you came back in twenty minutes you'd get the same reading. This is a damn fine thing.

—"Polling," November 13, 1948; *Writings from* The New Yorker, *1925–1976,* p. 60.

Pollution

(see Nature)

Possessions

Several months ago, finding myself in possession of one hundred and seventeen chairs divided about evenly between a city house and a country house, and desiring to simplify my life, I sold half of my worldly goods, evacuated the city house, gave up my employment, and came to live in New England. The difficulty of getting rid of even one half of one's possessions is considerable, even at removal prices. And after the standard items are disposed of—china, rugs, furniture, books—the surface is merely scratched: you open a closet door and there in the half-dark sit a catcher's mitt and an old biology notebook.

—"Removal," July 1938; *One Man's Meat*, p. 1.

I discovered by test that fully ninety per cent of whatever was on my desk as any given moment were IN things. Only ten percent were OUT things—almost too few to warrant a special container. This, in general, must be true of other people's lives too. It is the reason lives get so cluttered up—so many things (except money) filtering in, so few things (except strength) draining out.

—"Incoming Basket," July 1938; *One Man's Meat*, p. 9.

"A rat never knows when something is going to come in handy. I never throw anything away."

—*Charlotte's Web* (spoken by Templeton the rat), 1952, p. 74.

Acquisition goes on night and day—smoothly, subtly, imperceptibly. I have no sharp taste for acquiring things, but it is not necessary to desire things in order to acquire them. Goods and chattel seek a man out; they find him even though his guard is up. Books and oddities arrive in the mail. Gifts arrive on anniversaries and fête days. Veterans send ball point pens. Banks send memo books. If you happen to be a writer, readers send whatever may be cluttering up their own lives. I had a man once send me a chip of wood that showed the marks of a beaver's teeth. Someone dies, and a little trickle of indestructible keepsakes appears, to swell the flood. This steady influx is not counterbalanced by any comparable outgo. Under ordinary circumstances, the only stuff that leaves a home is paper trash and garbage; everything else stays on and digs in.

—"Good-Bye to 48th Street," November 12, 1957; *Points of My Compass*, p. 126, and *Essays of E. B. White*, p. 4.

Whenever anybody in America finds something on his desk or in his shelves that he wants to get rid of, he sends it to me. I just take everything to the attic and wait patiently for the house to catch fire.

—Letter to Jane Lightfoot (Mrs. Charles Hicks) Beaumont, September 6, 1980; *Letters of E. B. White*, Rev. Ed., p. 636.

Possessions breed like mice. A man forgets what a raft of irrelevant junk he has collected about him till he tries to move it.

—"Moving," October 5, 1935; *Writings from* The New Yorker, *1925–1976*, p. 199.

Prejudice

Nothing ever is written that is without slant and bias, because whatever is written is the result of the character, the dreams, the schemes, and the oddities of the man who writes it.

—"Talk of the Town," October 25, 1952; *The New Yorker*.

Pseudonyms

In the course of what passes for my career, I submitted pieces under twenty-five names other than my own. As I recall it, I sometimes signed a pseudonym when I found a piece wanting in merit, or virtue. I wanted the name "E. B. White" to be associated with excellence— literary splendor. It is possible that I once sent in a piece to the *NYer* signed with a phony name to see if I could get a rejection instead of an acceptance, but I have no clear recollection of having done that. I wouldn't put it past me, though. I was a fidgety young man, worried about all sorts of real and imaginary failings.

    —Letter to Eugene Kincaid, April 1981; *Letters of E. B. White*, Rev. Ed., p. 640.

[At] the early *New Yorker*...I was often either anonymous or pseud- onymous. At a certain period of my life I apparently had the annoying habit of changing my signature almost daily.

    —"Preface," *E. B. White, A Bibliographic Catalogue*, by Katharine Ro- mans Hall, p. x.

Public Speaking

As a child I was told that I should be seen and not heard. As an adult, I am making sure that I will be heard and not seen.

    —Unpublished letter to Mrs. A. H. Kimball, December 20, 1954; The E. B. White Collection, Carl A. Kroch Library, Cornell University, Ithaca, NY.

Today I was asked to read from my works at the Festival of the Arts in the White House, June 14. A Mr. Goldman had called *The New Yorker*, and Harriet had refused to give him my phone number here—which I thought comical. I had to call and say that I couldn't do it. But I doubt that he believed me; and I think very few people have any conception of my inability to make any sort of public appearance. They think it a pose or an evasion.

—Unpublished journal entry, May 20, 1965, 10:30 p.m.; White Literary LLC.

Quotations

Watch out for quoters, particularly for those who quote from Sir Walter Scott. "Oh what a tangled web we weave..." Poppycock. My friend the spider, here, practices to deceive every day of her life, but she doesn't weave a tangled web. Look at it!

—"Goings on in the Barnyard," by E. B. White,* August 15, 1973; *New York Times.*

* This was set up as a mock interview about Watergate, and it is the goose who is speaking here. The accompanying illustration pictured a silhouette of White, pencil and pad in hand, kneeling in front of the goose he was interviewing about Richard Nixon, G. Gordon Liddy, Senator Sam Ervin (the "quoter") and others.

Railroads

If Maine's railroads are to stay alive and haul passengers, they will need help from villages, cities, the state, and the federal government, and I think they should get it. A state without rail service is a state that is coming apart at the seams, and when a train stops at a village depot anywhere in America and a passenger steps off, I think that village is in an enviable condition, even if the lone passenger turns out to be a bank robber who does nothing better than stir the air up for a little while. But I think railroads will have to help themselves, too. They should raise their sights, not their fares. And they should stop skulking in their tent, and instead, try to beat the motorcar at its own game, which, if I do not misread the signs, should get easier as the years go on.

—"The Railroad," January 28, 1960; *Points of My Compass*, pp. 167–168, and *Essays of E. B. White*, p. 217.

Train thoughts are best. The thoughts of travelers are long, long thoughts....In a parlor car the mind gets its second wind.

—"The Talk of the Town," January 2, 1932; *The New Yorker*.

Rats

"Have you got a rat's point of view?" asked Anthony. "You look a little like a rat."

"No," replied Stuart. "I have more the point of view of a mouse, which is very different. I see things whole. It's obvious to me that rats are underprivileged. They've never been able to get out in the open."

"Rats don't like the open," said Agnes Beretska.

"That's because whenever they come out, somebody socks them. Rats might like the open if they were allowed to use it."

—*Stuart Little*, 1945, p. 94.

The rat had no morals, no conscience, no scruples, no consideration, no decency, no milk of rodent kindness, no compunctions, no higher feeling, no friendliness, no anything.

—*Charlotte's Web*, 1952, p. 46.

A rat is a rat.

—*Charlotte's Web*, 1952, p. 47.

As for Templeton, he's an old acquaintance and I know him well. He starts as a rat and he ends as a rat—the perfect opportunist and a great gourmand. I devoutly hope that you are not planning to elevate Templeton to sainthood.

—Letter to Gene Deitch,* January 12, 1971; *Letters of E. B. White*, Rev. Ed., p. 562.

* Deitch was Director of the film version of *Charlotte's Web* for Sagittarius Productions.

Reading
(see also Books)

In schools and colleges, in these audio-visual days, doubt has been raised as to the future of reading—whether the printed word is on its last legs. One college president has remarked that in fifty years "only five per cent of the people will be reading." ... To us it would seem that even if only one person out of a hundred and fifty million should continue as a *reader*, he would be the one worth saving, the nucleus around which to found a university.

—"The Future of Reading," March 24, 1951; *Second Tree from the Corner*, pp. 160–161.

Reading is the work of the alert mind, is demanding, and under ideal conditions produces finally a sort of ecstasy.

—"The Future of Reading," March 24, 1951; *Second Tree from the Corner*, p. 161.

As in the sexual experience, there are never more than two persons present in the act of reading—the writer, who is the impregnator, and the reader, who is the respondent. This gives the experience of reading a sublimity and power unequalled by any other form of communication.
——"The Future of Reading," March 24, 1951; *Second Tree from the Corner*, p. 161.

Readers and writers are scarce, as are publishers and reporters. The reports we get nowadays are those of men who have not gone to the scene of the accident, which is always further inside one's own head than it is convenient to penetrate without galoshes.
——"The Future of Reading," March 24, 1951; *Second Tree from the Corner*, p. 161.

It's an ironical twist of fate that my eyesight is failing just as I was about to sit down and read all the books I've never read. I had hoped to become literary just as I was crossing the finish line. But it's too late now. Can't see to do it. I did read Huckleberry Finn once, years ago, you will be relieved to know. And two years ago I began A. Karenina and finished it fourteen months later.
——Letter to Scott Elledge, May 25, 1982; *Letters of E. B. White*, Rev. Ed., p. 648.

Religion
(see also Faith)

I hope that Belief never is made to appear mandatory. One of our founders, in 1787, said, "Even the diseases of the people should be represented." Those were strange, noble words, and they have endured. They were on television yesterday. I distrust the slightest hint

172

of standard for political rectitude, knowing that it will open the way for persons in authority to set arbitrary standards of human behavior.

—"A Letter from the East: Bedfellows," February 6, 1956; *Points of My Compass*, p. 45, and *Essays of E. B. White*, p. 86.

Any religious ceremony in a public school is an exercise in orthodoxy—the orthodoxy of the Christian faith, which is correct for most of us, unacceptable to some. In an atmosphere of "voluntary" prayer, pupils coming from homes where other faiths prevail will feel an embarrassment by their non-participation; in the eyes of their schoolmates they will be "queer" or "different" or "irreligious." Such a stigma for a child can be emotionally disturbing, and although we no longer hang and burn our infidels and our witches, a schoolchild who is left out in the cold during a prayer session suffers scars that are very real.*

—Letter to Senator Margaret Chase Smith, August 15, 1966; *Letters of E. B. White*, Rev. Ed., p. 495.

* Re: The proposed Dirksen amendment.

For the most part, religion is tucked away in a bottom drawer, among the things we love but never use.

—"Sabbath Morn," February 1939; *One Man's Meat*, p. 41.

The Lord is persistent and lingers in strange places. He enjoys an honorable position among typographers, for He is always upper case. He enjoys a unique legal status, too, in the "Acts of God" code, where elemental violence affords exemption from responsibility.

—"Sabbath Morn," February 1939; *One Man's Meat*, p. 41.

When I feel sick unto death, I cry out in agony to God; when I speak boastingly, I knock on wood. Here is a clear case of divided responsibility, for there appears to be for me a power in wood that God doesn't possess.

—"Sabbath Morn," February 1939; *One Man's Meat,* pp. 40–41.

Ross, Harold
(see also *The New Yorker* and Thurber, James)

I am still encouraged to go on.* I wouldn't know where else to go.

—"The Art of the Essay, No. I, E. B. White," interview with George A. Plimpton and Frank H. Crowther, Fall 1969; *Paris Review,* Issue 48.

> * Harold Ross once commented on a piece White had written, saying, "I am encouraged to go on." In this interview, the *Paris Review* had asked if White was *still* encouraged to go on, as Ross had been.

But Ross didn't waste much time trying to corral "emerged" writers. He was looking for the ones that were found by turning over a stone.

—"The Art of the Essay, No. I, E. B. White," interview with George A. Plimpton and Frank H. Crowther, Fall 1969; *Paris Review,* Issue 48.

The only feud I recall* was the running battle between the editorial department and the advertising department. This was largely a one-sided affair, with the editorial department lobbing an occasional grenade into the enemy's lines just on general principles, to help them remember to stay out of sight. Ross was determined not to allow his magazine to be swayed, in the slightest degree, by the boys in advertising. As far as I know, he succeeded.

—"The Art of the Essay, No. I, E. B. White," interview with George A. Plimpton and Frank H. Crowther, Fall 1969; *Paris Review*, Issue 48.

* Referring to *The New Yorker* magazine.

Sailing
(see Boats and Boating)

Science

It seems as though no laws, not even fairly old ones, can safely be regarded as unassailable. The force of gravity, which we have always ascribed to the "pull of the earth," was reinterpreted the other day by a scientist who says that when we fall it is not earth pulling us, it is heaven pushing us. This blasts the rock on which we sit. If science can do a rightabout-face on a thing as fundamental as gravity, maybe Newton was a sucker not to have just eaten the apple.

—"Talk of the Town," April 3, 1937; *The New Yorker.*

Sea
(see also Boats and Boating)

The sound of the sea is the most time-effacing sound there is. The centuries reroll in a cloud and the earth becomes green again when you listen, with eyes shut, to the sea—a young green time when the water and the land were just getting acquainted and had known each other for only a few billion years and the mollusks were just beginning to dip and creep in the shallows.

— "On a Florida Key," February 1941; *Essays of E. B. White,* p. 141.

The sea answers all questions, and always in the same way; for when you read in the papers the interminable discussions and the bickering and the prognostications and the turmoil, the disagreements and the fateful decisions and agreements and the plans and the programs and the threats and counter threats, then you close your eyes and the sea dispatches one more big roller in the unbroken line since the beginning of the world and it combs and breaks and returns foaming and saying: "So soon?"

— "On a Florida Key," February 1941; *Essays of E. B. White,* p. 141.

When does a man quit the sea? How dizzy, how bumbling must he be? Does he quit while he's ahead, or wait till he makes some major mistake, like falling overboard or being flattened by an accidental jibe?

— "The Sea and the Wind That Blows," 1963; *Essays of E. B. White,* p. 207.

Seasons
(see also Weather)

Here in New England, each season carries a hundred foreshadowings of the season that is to follow—which is one of the things I love about it. Winter is rough and long, but spring lies all round about.

— "Home-Coming," December 10, 1955; *Points of My Compass,* p.33, and *Essays of E. B. White,* p. 12.

Yesterday, a small white keel feather escaped from my goose and lodged in the bank boughs near the kitchen porch, where I spied it as I came home in the cold twilight. The minute I saw the feather, I was projected into May, knowing a barn swallow would be along to claim the prize and use it to decorate the front edge of its nest. Immediately, the December air seemed full of wings of swallows and the warmth of barns.

—"Home-Coming," December 10, 1955; *Points of My Compass*, pp. 33–34, and *Essays of E. B. White*, p. 12.

Spring

A bulbous plant, the little crocus—
Always first in Spring to pocus
Head up.

—"Crocus," March 20, 1926; *The New Yorker*; *The Fox of Peapack*, p. 76.

The first sign of spring here is when the ice breaks up in the inkwell at the post office. A month later the ice leaves the lakes. And a month after that the first of the summer visitors shows up and the tax collector's wife removes the town records from her Frigidaire and plugs it in for the summer.

—"Town Meeting," March 1940; *One Man's Meat*, p. 123.

Earth is a hoyden, loud rejoice;
    Pigeon, sing cuccu!
The green girl, spring, has found her voice
    My heart is piercèd through.

The warm wind picketh winter's locks
    The jonquil bares his blade;

In Finley Shepard's window box
  The hyacinths parade.
  —"Pigeon, Sing Cuccu!" (excerpt), April 10, 1937; *The New Yorker.*

This is a day of high winds and extravagant promises, a day of bright skies and the sun on the white painted south sides of buildings, of lambs on the warm slope of the barnyard, their forelegs folded neatly and on their miniature faces a look of grave miniature content. Beneath the winter cover of spruce boughs the tulip thrusts its spear. A white hen is chaperoning thirteen little black chicks all over the place, showing them the world's fair with its lagoons and small worms. The wind is northwest and the bay is on the march.
  —"A Shepherd's Life," April 1940; *One Man's Meat,* p. 124.

No matter what changes take place in the world, or in me, nothing ever seems to disturb the face of spring.
  —"A Report in Spring," May 10, 1957; *Points of My Compass,* p. 112, and *Essays of E. B. White,* p. 15.

The smelts are running in the brooks. We had a mess for Monday lunch, brought to us by our son, who was fishing at two in the morning. At this season, a smelt brook is the nightclub of the town, and when the tide is a late one, smelting is for the young, who like small hours and late society.
  —"A Report in Spring," May 10, 1957; *Points of My Compass,* p. 112, and *Essays of E. B. White,* p. 15.

I find this morning that what I most vividly and longingly recall is the sight of my grandson and his little sunburnt sister returning to their kitchen door from an excursion, with trophies of the meadow clutched in their hands—she with a couple of violets, and smiling, he serious and holding dandelions, strangling them in a responsible grip. Children hold spring so tightly in their brown fists—just as grownups, who are less sure of it, hold it in their hearts.

    —"A Report in Spring," May 10, 1957; *Points of My Compass,* p. 114, and *Essays of E. B. White,* p. 16.

Summer

"Summertime is important. It's like a shaft of sunlight."

"Or a note in music," said Elizabeth Acheson.

"Or the way the back of a baby's neck smells if its mother keeps it tidy," said Marilyn Roberts.

Stuart sighed. "Never forget your summertimes, my dears," he said.

    —*Stuart Little,* 1945, p. 98.

"Have you got any sarsaparilla in your store?" asked Stuart. "I've got a ruinous thirst."

"Certainly," said the storekeeper. "Gallons of it. Sarsaparilla, root beer, birch beer, ginger ale, Moxie, lemon soda, Coca Cola, Pepsi Cola, Dipsi Cola, Pipsi Cola, Popsi Cola, and raspberry cream tonic. Anything you want."

"Let me have a bottle of sarsaparilla, please," said Stuart, "and a paper cup."

    —*Stuart Little,* 1945, p. 102.

The sound of victrola music right after breakfast gives the summer day a loose, footless feeling, the sort of inner sadness I have experienced on the outskirts of small towns on Sunday afternoon, or in the deserted city during a holiday, or on beaches where the bathhouses smelled of sour towels and yesterday's levity.

    —"Hot Weather," July 1939; *One Man's Meat,* p. 71.

Summertime, oh, summertime, pattern of life indelible, the fade-proof lake, the woods unshatterable, the pasture with the sweetfern and the juniper forever and ever, summer without end; this was the background, and the life along the shore was the design, the cottagers with their innocent and tranquil design, their tiny docks with the flagpole and the American flag floating against the white clouds in the blue sky, the little paths over the roots of the trees leading from camp to camp and the paths leading back to the outhouses and the can of lime for sprinkling, and at the souvenir counters at the store the miniature birch-bark canoes and the postcards that showed things looking a little better than they looked. This was the American family at play.

    —"Once More to the Lake," August 1941; *Essays of E. B. White*, p. 200.

It seemed to me, as I kept remembering all this, that those times and those summers had been infinitely precious and worth saving. There had been jollity and peace and goodness.

    —"Once More to the Lake," August 1941; *Essays of E. B. White*, p. 200.

In summertime, cars pass slowly by the house, with people gaping to see where America's oldest living author lives and sulks. In summertime, bad boys on fast motorcycles roar by at naptime, and the phone rings and it is a man calling from a bar in Palo Alto or a bar in La Jolla to tell me that he is in tears because of something I wrote in 1937. (He has had three martinis and could easily break down from reading a Macy ad.) In summertime, my boat hangs idle at her mooring because I am subject to dizzy spells and prefer to have them on land.

    —Letter to Ann Honeycutt, September 15, 1979; *Letters of E. B. White*, Rev. Ed., p. 629.

Autumn

Florida is a wasteland as a result of the Great Freeze of last fall. Almost all of the Australian pines (tall feathery, handsome trees) were killed. The sea grapes are gone and the punk trees and the coconut palms and the Royal palms and the banyans. Even the mangroves, which live with their feet in the water are about half dead—Orange trees and grapefruit trees are loaded with frozen fruit; they stand in the groves looking like wild apple trees on a December morn in Maine. Nothing has been cut down yet—everyone is waiting to see which tree will come back, if any, and also everyone awaits the appraiser, who will estimate the amount of storm damage for tax write-off. But despite the dreary prospect I think it won't be long before the jungle asserts itself and grows lush again.

  —Letter to Allene White, January 15, 1964; *Letters of E. B. White*, Rev. Ed., p. 466.

The coming of fall has a tonic effect on me. Summer is the bad time for me, with its sad afternoons and partially insane visitors—most of them strangers. Even with Christmas looming, I feel that if I can just get through summer, I've got it licked for another year.

  —Letter to Ann Honeycutt, September 15, 1979; *Letters of E. B. White*, Rev. Ed., p. 629.

Winter

Just to live in New England in winter is a full-time job; you don't have to "do" anything. The idle pursuit of making-a-living is pushed to one side, where it belongs, in favor of living itself, a task of such immediacy, variety, beauty, and excitement that one is powerless to resist its wild embrace.

  —"A Report in Winter," January 30, 1958; *Points of My Compass*, p. 131.

At this season of the year, darkness is a more insistent thing than cold. The days are short as any dream.

—"A Report in Winter," January 30, 1958; *Points of My Compass,* p. 137.

I like to come in from chores and find the early dark in the rooms, when the only gleam is a single lamp over an amaryllis bulb on which my wife is practicing some sort of deception. I like groping my way into the barn cellar at six, where my two whiteface heifers are feeding at the rack, their great white heads visible, their dark bodies invisible— just two heads suspended in air, as neatly as John the Baptist's.

—"A Report in Winter," January 30, 1958; *Points of My Compass,* p. 137.

I didn't care for athletics, being skinny and small, but I liked ice ponds and skating, and on winter afternoons and evenings I would visit a pond (a fifteen-minute ride on a trolley car) and skate with a girl named Mildred Hesse. Her eyes were blue and her ankles were strong. Together we must have covered hundreds of miles, sometimes leaving the pond proper and gliding into the woods on narrow fingers of ice. We didn't talk much, never embraced, we just skated for the ecstasy of skating—a magical glide. After one of these sessions, I would go home and play Liebestraum on the Autola, bathed in the splendor of perfect love and natural fatigue. This brief interlude on ice, in the days of my youth, had a dreamlike quality, a purity, that has stayed with me all my life; and when nowadays I see a winter sky and feel the wind dropping with the sun and the naked trees against a reddening west, I remember what it was like to be in love before any of love's complexities or realities or disturbances had entered in, to dilute its splendor and challenge its perfection.

—"Mount Vernon," 1976; *Letters of E. B. White,* Rev. Ed., p. 10.

Security

I like to watch the faces of people who are trying to get up their nerve to take to the air. You see them at ticket booths in amusement parks, in the waiting room at the airport. Within them two irreconcilables are at war—the desire for safety, the yearning for a dizzy release.

—"Security," September 1938; *One Man's Meat,* p. 11.

Security, for me, took a tumble not when I read that there were Communists in Hollywood but when I read your editorial in praise of loyalty testing and thought control. If a man is in health, he doesn't need to take anyone else's temperature to know where he is going. If a newspaper or a motion picture company is in health, it can get rid of Communists and spies simply by reading proof and watching previews.

—Letter to the *New York Herald Tribune,* November 29, 1947; *Letters of E. B. White,* p. 267.

It is paradoxical that the more secure a person gets in a material way, the less secure he may become in other ways. The least secure fellows you see around, in any age or period, are the big fellows, with their personal empires and kingdoms and all the responsibilities and ulcers that go with kinging. In a sense, the only genuinely secure person is a healthy man possessed of absolutely nothing; such a man stands aloof and safe—there is no way either to reduce his fortune or to debase his currency. But even he is not perfectly secure: his loneliness may suddenly depress his spirit, and this might endanger his health.

—"Talk of the Town," November 20, 1948; *The New Yorker.*

Said Mr. A to Mr. B,
"I doubt the loyalty of C."

Said Mr. B to Mr. A,
"I'm shocked and stunned by what you say;
We'd better check on him today,
And since you've brought up Mr. C,
I feel that I must mention D.
I rather doubt *his* loyalty."
    —"The ABC of Security" (excerpt), May 9, 1953; *The New Yorker.*

Sex

I'm sorry for cows who have to boast
Of affairs they've had by parcel post,
I'm sorry for man with his plots and guile,
His test-tube manners, his test-tube smile;
I'll multiply and I'll increase
As I always have—by mere caprice;
For I am a queen and I am a bee,
I'm devil-may-care and I'm fancy-free,
Love-in-air is the thing for me,...
    —"Song of the Queen Bee," *Second Tree from the Corner,* p. 207, and
    Poems and Sketches of E. B. White, 1981, p. 194.

We were determined that sex should retain its high spirits. So we
decided to spoof the medical books and, incidentally, to have a quick
look at love and passion.
    —"Introduction," 1950, *Is Sex Necessary?,* by James Thurber and
    E. B. White, 2004 Ed., p. 4.

Skating

Skating after you've had a couple of hot rums takes on a new quality, new dimensions. Whoever would have imagined that Mr. Rockefeller, the teetotaler, by joining steel and rum would have thus emancipated his compatriots? At night, with a waltz playing, the dark spruces towering above your head, and the R.C.A. Building shooting straight aloft beyond the spruces, the pond is a page out of a fairy tale.

—"Notes and Comment," January 6, 1937; *The New Yorker.*

Skating on the frog pond under an early rising moon, I am conscious of the promise of polliwogs under my runners, and my thoughts turn to seeds and the germinal prospect.

—"Salt Water Farm," January, 1939; *One Man's Meat,* p. 31.

Society

The sexual revolution began with Man's discovery that he was not attractive to Woman, as such. The lion had his mane, the peacock his gorgeous plumage, but Man found himself in a three-button sack suit. His masculine appearance not only failed to excite Woman, but in many cases it only served to bore her. The result was that Man found it necessary to develop attractive personal traits to offset his dull appearance. He learned to say funny things. He learned to smoke, and blow smoke rings. He learned to earn money.

—*Is Sex Necessary?,* by James Thurber and E. B. White, 2004 Ed., p. 82.

Man's so wise he is growing foolish,
Some of his schemes are downright ghoulish;

He owns a bomb that'll end creation
And he wants to change the sex relation.
—"Song of the Queen Bee," December 15, 1945; *Second Tree from
the Corner*, p. 206, and *Poems and Sketches of E. B. White*, 1981, p. 193.

A prude is a lady whose
Sense of propriety
Marches ahead of the
State of society.
—"Prude" (excerpt), November 14, 1925; *The New Yorker.*

When I was a child people simply looked about them and were moderately happy; today they peer beyond the seven seas, bury themselves waist deep in tidings, and by and large what they see and hear makes them unutterably sad.
—"Removal," July 1938; *One Man's Meat*, p. 3.

I lived in an age when parents weren't scared of their children; they commanded respect, enforced discipline and maintained an orderly household. It can still be done, but the motor car and the TV have clearly added to the burden of the task of discipline and of communication.
—"E. B. White: Notes and Comment by Author," interview with Israel Shenker, July 11, 1969; *New York Times.*

Sailors have an expression about the weather: they say, the weather is a great bluffer. I guess the same is true of our human society—things can look dark, then a break shows in the clouds, and all is changed, sometimes rather suddenly. It is quite obvious that the human race has made a queer mess of life on this planet. But as a people we probably harbor seeds of goodness that have lain for a long time, waiting to

sprout when the conditions are right. Man's curiosity, his relentlessness, his inventiveness, his ingenuity have led him into deep trouble.
We can only hope that these same traits will enable him to claw his
way out.

—Letter to Mr. Nadeau, March 30, 1973; *Letters of E. B. White*, Rev.
Ed., p. 596.

Madam! Lady! Baby doll!
This is what the world objects to:
Must you smell up all the hall
  Just to charm the guy you're next to?
    You were lost on him already.

—"To a Perfumed Lady at the Concert" (excerpt), March 19,
1932; *The New Yorker*.

The 1920s was a gaudy decade that I don't need to tell you about....It's
as though you were writing about the millions of modern young cou-
ples by describing them as "living in sin" when what they are doing of
course, is living a la mode. The 1920s was an explosive period of social
breakdown into which almost all who lived at that time got drawn.
Prohibition really triggered it, with its bootleggers and speakeasies, so
that everyone was breaking the law when he sat down to a meal. Over
in the North River, the transatlantic liners sounded their horns of
departure, and the citizens listened uneasily to this midnight invitation
to revelry, debauchery, and escape.

—Letter to Scott Elledge, June 16, 1982; *Letters of E. B. White*, Rev.
Ed., pp. 653–654.

Here's a report from Minneapolis, home of the Twins. A mother of
two...who works in a bookstore, says the ELEMENTS* is propped
up on the front table with all the other hot paperbacks—between the

Rand McNally Road Atlas and *The Joy of Sex*—and is selling faster than either of them. Actually, it's scary to learn that the country is turning from sex to semicolons. Makes me uneasy.

—Letter to D. Anthony English, July 20, 1979; *Letters of E. B. White*, Rev. Ed, p. 628.

   * *The Elements of Style.*

Spelling

"Well," said Stuart, "a misspelled word is an abomination in the sight of everyone."

—*Stuart Little*, 1945, p. 90.

If you go about among the intelligentsia it is always good to know ten words nobody can spell. The best list we know of is as follows: supersede, naphtha, tranquillity;* liquefy; sacrilegious, kimono, paraffin, rarefy, picnicking, and battalion. The common variety of mortal, confronted with this list, either spells all ten wrong or blunders into a possible two out of ten. A little astuteness in laying wagers, and this list should take anyone through a long winter.

—"Notes and Comment: Bee," October 20, 1928; *The New Yorker*.

   * Tranquility can also be spelled with one l...but it was written here with two.

Spiders

Spiders expect to have their webs busted, and they take it in their stride. One of Charlotte's daughters placed her web in the tie-ups, right behind my bull calf, and I kept forgetting about it and would bust one of her foundation lines on my trips to and from the trapdoor where I push manure into the cellar.... After several days of this, during which she had to rebuild the entire web each evening, she solved the matter neatly by changing the angle of the web so that the foundation line no longer crossed my path. Her ingenuity has impressed me, and I am now teaching her to write SOME BOOK, and will let Brentano have her for their window.

—Letter quoted in "Stuart, Wilbur, Charlotte: A Tale of Tales," by Ursula Nordstrom, May 12, 1974; *New York Times.*

It seems to us the Stock Market has outgrown its present physical organization. Since it has become the pastime of the nation, it should begin to offer something in the way of adequate seating capacity and convenient hours. A little showmanship would help. It should be open at night, and it should operate in some place like Madison Square Garden or the Yankee Stadium, and it should be broadcast.

—"Notes and Comment," June 29, 1929; *The New Yorker.*

Spring
(see Seasons)

Style
(see also Grammar, Language)

The public is just the whipping boy for the industry's style experts, who are trying to out-streamline each other and who are so snarled up in their little chromium do-funnies and nutty refinements to take the eye of half-anesthetized people in the sluggish air of a salesroom that they are not doing their job as engineers.

—"Department of Correction, Amplification, and Abuse," March 6, 1937; *The New Yorker.*

Young writers often suppose that style is a garnish for the meat of prose, a sauce by which a dull dish is made palatable. Style has no such separate entity. The beginner should approach style warily, realizing that it is himself he is approaching, no other; and he should begin by turning resolutely away from all devices that are popularly believed to indicate style—all mannerisms, tricks, adornments. The approach to style is by way of plainness, simplicity, orderliness, sincerity.

—*The Elements of Style*, 1959; 2nd Ed., 1972, p. 62.

When corset was a common noun
More feminine than neuter,
A whale was very glad to die
To make a woman cuter.

But now that corset's obsolete
Through Woman's latest notion,
A whale may swim the live-long day
Down in the deep blue ocean.

—"Definitions: Corset," November 7, 1925; *The New Yorker.*

A single overstatement, wherever or however it occurs, diminishes the whole, and a carefree superlative has the power to destroy, for the reader, the object of the writer's enthusiasm.

—"An Approach to Style," *The Elements of Style*, 1959; 2nd Ed., 1972, p. 65.

Do not affect a breezy manner. The volume of writing is enormous, these days, and much of it has a sort of windiness about it, almost as though the author were in a state of euphoria.

—"An Approach to Style," *The Elements of Style*, 1959; 2nd Ed., 1972, p. 66.

Be obscure clearly. Be wild of tongue in a way we can understand.
—"An Approach to Style," *The Elements of Style*, 1959; 2nd Ed.,
1972, p. 72.

When you become hopelessly mired in a sentence, it is best to start
fresh; do not try to fight your way through against the terrible odds
of syntax.
—"An Approach to Style," *The Elements of Style*, 1959; 2nd Ed.,
1972, p. 72.

Summer
(see Seasons)

Symbolism

There are always people who find symbolism in everything they read,
and perhaps they are right. But in the case of "Charlotte's Web," if
you enjoyed it as a simple tale of country matters, I think you were on
course. It is that to me, and nothing else. Having been quite intimately
acquainted with Charlotte herself, and some of her children, and lately
some of her grandchildren, I feel that I know what I am talking about.
—Unpublished letter to Mrs. Mary Risch, April 14, 1954; The
E. B. White Collection, Carl A. Kroch Library, Cornell University, Ithaca, NY.

The interpretation of my "Letter from the East"* by one of your pupils is quite staggering. But you can tell her that I probably wouldn't
be able to do any better myself. You can also say that there are no
symbols in the piece, to my knowledge. Why does everyone search so
diligently for symbols these days? It is a great vogue. Fred symbolizing

"the government as a whole" is such a terrifying idea that I am still shaking all over from fright—the way he used to shake from the excitement of anticipation.

> —Letter to Lorlyn L. Thatcher, April 23, 1956; *Letters of E. B. White*, Rev. Ed., p. 384.
>
> * Of February 18, 1956.

It is an extraordinary document,* any way you look at it, and it makes me realize how lucky I was (when I was writing the book) that I didn't know what in hell was going on.

> —Letter to Peter Neumeyer, *The Annotated Charlotte's Web*, Introduction and Notes, by Peter F. Neumeyer, 1994, p. xv.
>
> * A scholarly analysis of *Charlotte's Web*.

Taxes

We have given about a year's thought to the withholding principle of taxation (not to be confused with the pay-as-you-go plan) and are now ready with our conclusion. Our belief is that withholding is a bad way to go about collecting tax money, even though the figures may show that it gets results. It is bad because it implies that the individual is incapable of handling his own affairs.

> —"Withholding," February 5, 1944; *Second Tree from the Corner*, p. 123, and *Notes on Our Times*, p. 77.

Telephone

I don't really think fast enough to be allowed to use the telephone.

> —Letter to William Maxwell, November 19, 1971; *Letters of E. B. White*, Rev. Ed., p. 579.

Television

(see also Entertainment)

The news of television, however, is what I particularly go for when I get a chance at the paper, for I believe television is going to be the test of the modern world, and that in this new opportunity to see beyond the range of our vision we shall discover either a new and unbearable disturbance of the general peace or a saving radiance in the sky. We shall stand or fall by television—of that I am quite sure.
  —"Removal," July 1938; *One Man's Meat,* p. 2.

Television will enormously enlarge the eye's range, and, like radio, will advertise the Elsewhere. Together with the tabs, the mags, and the movies, it will insist that we forget the primary and near in favor of the secondary and the remote. More hours in every twenty-four will be spent digesting ideas, sounds, images—distant and concocted. In sufficient accumulation, radio sounds and television sights may become more familiar to us than their originals. A door closing, heard over the air; a face contorted, seen in a panel of light—these will emerge as the real and the true; and when we bang the door of our own cell or look into another's face the impression will be of mere artifice.
  —"Removal," July 1938; *One Man's Meat,* p. 3.

In answer to your direct question, I wasn't satisfied with "Stuart Little" on TV, but I didn't expect to be. It came out about the way I figured it would.... It is the fixed purpose of television and motion pictures to scrap the author, sink him without a trace, on the theory that he is incompetent, has never read his own stuff, is not responsible for anything he ever wrote, and wouldn't know what to do about it even if he were.
  —Letter to Harriet Walden, March 1966; *Letters of E. B. White,* Rev. Ed., p. 490.

Non-commercial TV should address itself to the idea of excellence, not the idea of acceptability—which is what keeps commercial TV from climbing the staircase. I think TV should be providing the visual counterpart of the literary essay, should arouse our dreams, satisfy our hunger for beauty, take us on journeys, enable us to participate in events, present great drama and music, explore the sea and the sky and woods and the hills. It should be our Lyceum, our Chautauqua, our Minsky's, and our Camelot. It should restate and clarify the social dilemma and the political pickle. Once in a while it does, and you get a quick glimpse of its potential.

　　—Letter to the Carnegie Commission, 1967; *Letters of E. B. White*, Rev. Ed., pp. 495–496.

Television affects the style of children—that I know. I receive letters from children, and many of them begin: "Dear Mr. White, My name is Donna Reynolds." This is the Walter Cronkite gambit, straight out of TV. When I was a child I never started a letter, "My name is Elwyn White." I simply signed my name at the end.

　　—"The Art of the Essay, No. I, E. B. White," interview with George A. Plimpton and Frank H. Crowther, Fall 1969; *Paris Review*, Issue 48.

Terror
(see Atomic Age)

Thoreau, Henry David

A person who is about to encounter the text of "Walden" for the first time should buy a small unadorned edition, such as the

pocket Oxford, which will allow him to travel light and on a high plane.
  —"Walden," December 28, 1946; *Writings from* The New Yorker, *1925–1976*, p. 41.

The Thoreau Society wants contributions so it can buy the house at 73 Main Street, Concord, where Henry David Thoreau sat taking pot shots at the whole theory of shelter. We haven't decided yet whether to listen to the Society or to Henry.
  —"Thoreau and Shelter," August 7, 1948; *Writings from* The New Yorker, *1925–1976*, p. 42.

Henry Thoreau has probably been more wildly misconstrued than any other person of comparable literary stature. He got a reputation for being a naturalist, and he was not much of a naturalist. He got a reputation for being a hermit, and he was no hermit. He was a writer, is what he was.
  —"The Individualist," May 7, 1949; *Writings from* The New Yorker, *1925–1976*, p. 39.

Walden is the only book I own, although there are some others unclaimed on my shelves. Every man, I think, reads one book in his life, and this is mine. It is not the best book I ever encountered, perhaps, but it is for me the handiest, and I keep it about me in much the same way one carries a handkerchief—for relief in moments of defluxion or despair.
  —"Visitors to the Pond," May 23, 1953; *Writings from* The New Yorker, *1925–1976*, pp. 44–45.

I think it is of some advantage to encounter the book* at a period in one's life when the normal anxieties and enthusiasms and rebellions of youth closely resemble those of Thoreau in that spring of 1845 when he borrowed an ax, went out to the woods, and began to whack down some trees for timber. Received at such a juncture, the book is like an invitation to life's dance, assuring the troubled recipient that no matter what befalls him in the way of success or failure he will always be welcome at the party—that the music is played for him, too, if he will but listen and move his feet. In effect, that is what the book is—an invitation, unengraved; and it stirs one as a young girl is stirred by her first big party bid.

> —"A Slight Sound at Evening," Summer 1954; *Points of My Compass*, pp. 15–16, and *Essays of E. B. White*, p. 234.
>
> * The book, *Walden*, was published in 1854. This was written in honor of its 100th anniversary.

If our colleges and universities were alert, they would present a cheap pocket edition of the book [Thoreau's *Walden*] to every senior upon graduating, along with his sheepskin, or instead of it. Even if some senior were to take it literally and start felling trees, there could be worse mishaps: the ax is older than the Dictaphone and it is just as well for a young man to see what kind of chips he leaves before listening to the sound of his own voice.

> —"A Slight Sound at Evening," 1954; *Points of My Compass*, p. 16, and *Essays of E. B. White*, p. 235.

And even if some [readers of *Walden*] were to get no farther than the table of contents, they would learn how to name eighteen chapters by the use of only thirty-nine words and would see how sweet are the uses of brevity.

> —"A Slight Sound at Evening," 1954; *Points of My Compass*, p. 16, and *Essays of E. B. White*, p. 235.

Thurber, James
(see also *The New Yorker*)

He* was not a man who carried a camera. He carried a pencil that put
a camera to shame.
—Letter to Scott Elledge, October 27, 1982; *Letters of E. B. White*,
Rev. Ed., p. 658.
* Thurber.

To understand, even vaguely, Thurber's art, it is necessary to grasp
the two major themes which underlie all his drawings. The first theme
is what I call the "melancholy of sex"; the other is what I can best
describe as the "implausibility of animals." These two basic ideas mo-
tivate, subconsciously, his entire creative life.
—"A Note on the Drawings in This Book," *Is Sex Necessary?*, by
James Thurber and E. B. White, 2004 Ed., p. 179.

When one studies the drawings, it soon becomes apparent that a
strong undercurrent of grief runs through them. In almost every instance the *man* in the picture is badly frightened, or even hurt.
—"A Note on the Drawings in This Book," *Is Sex Necessary?*, by
James Thurber and E. B. White, 2004 Ed., p. 179.

I am one of the lucky ones. I knew him before blindness hit him, before
fame hit him, and I tend always to think of him as a young artist in a small
office in a big city, with all the world still ahead. It was a fine thing to be
young and at work in New York for a new magazine when Thurber was
young and at work,* and I will always be glad that this happened to me.
—"James Thurber," *The New Yorker* obituary, November 11, 1961;
reprinted in *Writings from* The New Yorker, *1925–1976*, p. 233.
* White and James Thurber shared an office at *The New
Yorker* for many years, including the months in 1929 when

they co-authored *Is Sex Necessary? Or Why We Feel the Way We Do.*

The copy paper disappeared at a scandalous rate—not because our production was high (although it was) but because Thurber used copy paper as the natural receptacle for discarded sorrows, immediate joys, stale dreams, golden prophecies, and messages of good cheer to the outside world and to fellow-workers.

   —"James Thurber," *The New Yorker* obituary, November 11, 1961; reprinted in *Writings from* The New Yorker, *1925–1976,* pp. 233–234.

His mind was never at rest, and his pencil was connected to his mind by the best connective tissue I have ever seen in action.

   —"James Thurber," *The New Yorker* obituary, November 11, 1961; reprinted in *Writings from* The New Yorker, *1925–1976,* p. 234.

During his happiest years, Thurber did not write the way a surgeon operates, he wrote the way a child skips rope, the way a mouse waltzes.

   —"James Thurber," *The New Yorker* obituary, November 11, 1961; reprinted in *Writings from* The New Yorker, *1925–1976,* p. 234.

My deadline now is death. Thurber once said it's remarkable how many people are up and around.

   —"E. B. White: Notes and Comment by Author," interview with Israel Shenker, July 11, 1969; *New York Times.*

Time
(see also Fatherhood, Future)

Eastern Standard
The Time of My Life

I wake, the same as always,
   To find the east is gray,
And night, in a thousand small ways,
   Surrendering to day.

My clock, that once could rouse me
   And rush me to the street,
One gorgeous hour allows me—
   Legitimate and sweet.
   —"Eastern Standard: The Time of My Life," September 25,
   1926; *The New Yorker.*

I find that I still hold to the same opinions that were mine when I
was thirteen. I think a man should learn to swim in the pool of time,
should tuck up his affairs so they fit into a canoe, and having snugged
all down, should find out what bird is his eagle, and climb the tree.
   —"Stratagem for Retirement," quoted in *E. B. White,* by Edward C.
   Sampson, p. 57.

War
(see also Peace)

The answer to war is no war.
   —"Preface," 1946; *The Wild Flag,* p. ix.

One of the most time-consuming things is to have an enemy.
   —"A Report in Winter," January 30, 1958; *Points of My Compass,* p.
   132, and *Essays of E. B. White,* p. 47.

The likeliest means of removing war from the routine of national life
is to elevate the community's authority to a level which is above the
national level.
   —"Preface," 1946; *The Wild Flag,* p. ix.

War is becoming increasingly unpopular with warriors. We needn't set too much store by this; nevertheless, it is stimulating to learn that the ones who have been doing the fighting have an extremely low opinion of the whole business. If war were only mildly unpopular, one might despair of ever getting rid of it down the drain. But war has reached a new low in the esteem of all people. The bombing of cities has made every citizen a participant in war, and this has swelled the ranks of war's detractors.

—"Preface," 1946; *The Wild Flag*, pp. xiii–xiv.

Americans are willing to go to enormous trouble and expense defending their principles with arms, very little trouble and expense advocating them with words. Temperamentally we are ready to die for certain principles (or, in the case of overripe adults, send youngsters to die), but we show little inclination to advertise the reasons for dying.

—"The Thud of Ideas," September 23, 1950; *The New Yorker*.

The world organization debates disarmament in one room and, in the next room, moves the knights and pawns that make national arms imperative.

—"Sootfall and Fallout," October 18, 1956; *Points of My Compass*, p. 85, and *Essays of E. B. White*, p. 96.

A popular belief these days is that the clue to peace is in disarmament. Pick a statesman of any stature in any nation and he will almost certainly tell you that a reduction in arms is the gateway to peace. Unfortunately, disarmament doesn't have much to do with peace. I sometimes wish it had, it enjoys such an excellent reputation and commands such a lot of attention. Keeping itself strong is always a nation's first concern whenever arms are up for discussion, and disarmament is simply one of the devices by which a nation tries to increase its strength relative to the strength of others. On this naked earth, a nation that approaches disarmament as though it were a humanitarian ideal is either suffering from delusions or planning a deception.

—"Unity," June 4, 1960; *Points of My Compass*, pp. 178–179, and *Essays of E. B. White*, p. 102.

I am afraid that blaming armaments for war is like blaming fever for disease.

—"Unity," June 4, 1960; *Points of My Compass*, p. 179, and *Essays of E. B. White*, p. 102.

Total disarmament would not leave anyone free of the threat of war, it would simply leave everyone temporarily without the help of arms in the event of war.

—"Unity," June 4, 1960; *Points of My Compass*, p. 179, and *Essays of E. B. White*, p. 102.

Weather
(see also Seasons)

One afternoon while we were there at that lake a thunderstorm came up. It was like the revival of an old melodrama that I had seen long ago with childish awe.... Afterward the calm, the rain steadily rustling in the calm lake, the return of light and hope and spirits, and the campers running out in joy and relief to go swimming in the rain, their bright cries perpetuating the deathless joke about how they were getting simply drenched, and the children screaming with delight at the new sensation of bathing in the rain, and the joke about getting drenched linking the generations in a strong indestructible chain. And the comedian who waded in carrying an umbrella.

—"Once More to the Lake," August 1941; *Essays of E. B. White*, p. 202.

Now all we need is a meteorologist who has once been soaked to the skin without ill effect. No one can write knowingly of the weather who walks bent over on wet days.

   —"Dismal," February 25, 1950; *Writings from* The New Yorker, *1925–1976*, p. 7.

The weather has always played a big role in people's lives, and in the last ten years or so, thanks to radio and TV, the weather has rocketed to stardom. It is the Great White Topic. It haunts the airwaves and partakes of the spirit of evil.... the upshot of having weather presented by well-insulated broadcasters who seldom go out in it is that the public now regards inclemency as a personal affront.

   —"Notes and Comment," June 18, 1955; *The New Yorker.*

By far the best weathermen are fishermen; they don't always like the weather, but we've never yet heard one patronize it.

   —"Notes and Comment," June 18, 1955; *The New Yorker.*

    *   *   *

Asterisks? So soon?

    *   *   *

It is a hot-weather sign, the asterisk. The cicada of the typewriter, telling the long steaming noons.

   —"Hot Weather," July 1939; *One Man's Meat*, p. 71.

Winter
(see Seasons)

Words

Capturing a thought
And hoping to display it in words
Is like capturing a sea gull
And hoping to show its velvet flight
By stuffing it—wings outstretched—
And hanging it in a window
By a thread.

 —"Personal Column," March 31, 1923; *Seattle Times.*

Remind me to discuss the necessity for reviving the word piffle.

 —"Compost," June 1940; *One Man's Meat*, p. 131.

I wrote: "…a pretty good case can be made out for setting fire to it and starting fresh." Some studious person…came upon the word "fresh" and saw how easily it could be changed to the word "afresh," a simple matter of affixing an "a."…

 An afresh starter is likely to be a person who wants to get agoing. He doesn't just want to get going, he wants to get agoing. An afresh starter is also likely to be a person who feels acold when he steps out of the tub.

 Some of my best friends lie abed and run amuck, but they do not start afresh. Never do. However, if there is to be a growing tendency in *The New Yorker* office to improve words by affixing an "a," I shall try to adjust myself to this amusing situation. Characters in my stories will henceforth go afishing, and they will read *Field & Stream.* They will not be typical people, they will all be atypical. Some of them, perhaps all of them, will be asexual, even amoral.

 Amen.

 —Interoffice memo to William Shawn, February, 1945; *Letters of E. B. White,* Rev. Ed., pp. 249–250.

Templeton was down there now, rummaging around. When he returned to the barn, he carried in his mouth an advertisement he had torn from a crumpled magazine.

"How's this?" he asked, showing the ad to Charlotte.

"It says 'Crunchy.' 'Crunchy' would be a good word to write in your web."

"Just the wrong idea," replied Charlotte. "Couldn't be worse. We don't want Zuckerman to think Wilbur is crunchy. He might start thinking about crisp, crunchy bacon and tasty ham. That would put ideas into his head. We must advertise Wilbur's noble qualities, not his tastiness."

—*Charlotte's Web,* 1952, pp. 97–98.

I looked up "toll" in my Webster's and found that it derives from a Middle English verb tollen or tullen. The noun "toll," however, seems to be a different fish—goes back to the Greek telos, a tax. Well, it's nice to know that tolling a mackerel is Middle English and paying toll is Greek.

—Unpublished letter to Dr. Gray, July 11, 1965; in the White Literary LLC archive.

When my wife's Aunt Caroline was in her nineties, she lived with us, and she once remarked: "Remembrance is sufficient of the beauty we have seen." I cherish the remembrance of the beauty I have seen. I cherish the grave, compulsive word.

—"E. B. White: Notes and Comment by Author," interview with Israel Shenker, July 11, 1969; *New York Times.*

I fell in love with the sound of an early typewriter and have been stuck with it ever since. I believed then, as I do now, in the goodness of the published word: it seemed to contain an essential goodness, like the smell of leaf mold.

—"The Egg Is All," December 7, 1971; remarks on receiving the National Medal for Literature.

As for the old cob's* speech, his wordiness, there I think you are probably on solid ground. Father was quite a talker and didn't hesitate to say in twenty words what could be said in six.

—Letter to Scott Elledge, May 25, 1982; *Letters of E. B. White*, Rev. Ed, p. 650.

* Elledge, White's biographer, had surmised that the old cob (Louis's father) in *The Trumpet of the Swan* was modeled after White's own father and White allowed that this was probably true.

And a Word of Advice

The first time we heard the word "hopefully" used to mean something it doesn't mean was from the lips of a pretty woman whom we were wining and dining in a restaurant. We asked her when she expected to move into her apartment, and she answered, "Hopefully on Tuesday." We laid down our fork and asked her whether she meant "I hope on Tuesday" or whether she meant "On Tuesday in a hopeful frame of mind." She then laid down *her* fork and wanted to know what the hell we were driving at. She confessed that she saw nothing wrong with "Hopefully on Tuesday." Rather than labor the thing, we shifted subjects; it is not our policy to badger pretty women. Since that memorable occasion, we have encountered this use of "hopefully" at every turn. It is all over the place and has, we suspect, come into the language. *Time,* always elegant in its rhetoric, appeared not long ago with this sobering sentence: "The Government would like to bring the case to a quick trial, hopefully before the end of January." Lacking a fork to lay down, we simply laid down the magazine.

—"Notes and Comment," March 27, 1965; *The New Yorker.*

As for us, we would as lief Simonize our grandmother as personalize our writing.

—"Calculating Machine," March 3, 1951; *Second Tree From the Corner,* p. 166.

Words that are not used orally are seldom the ones to put on paper.

—"An Approach to Style," *The Elements of Style,* 1959; 2nd Ed., 1972, p. 68.

Adverbs are easy to build. Take an adjective or a participle, add -ly, and behold! You have an adverb. But you'd probably be better off without it. Do not write *tangledly.* The word itself is a tangle.

—"An Approach to Style," *The Elements of Style,* 1959; 2nd Ed., 1972, p. 68.

The young writer should learn to spot them—words that at first glance seem freighted with delicious meaning, but that soon burst in air, leaving nothing but a memory of bright sound.

—"An Approach to Style," *The Elements of Style,* 1959; 2nd Ed., 1972, p. 76.

Work

I have no heroes, no saints. I do have a tremendous respect for any-one who does something extremely well, no matter what. I would rather watch a really gifted plumber than listen to a bad poet. I'd rather watch someone build a good boat than attend the launching of a poorly constructed play. My admirations are wide-ranging and are not confined to arts and letters.

—"E. B. White: Notes and Comment by Author," interview with Israel Shenker, July 11, 1969; *New York Times.*

It has been a great satisfaction to me to have watched Joel work his way into the big time—which is excellence, no matter what the product is, or the craft, or the profession. I love boats without knowing much about them, and I was glad to find Joe pursuing the matter to the last ditch and the final hill, because that is where the fun is and the balm of accomplishment.

Your article,* so loaded with the mystique of wood and boats, will be an inspiration to anyone who respects the ideal of excellence in this increasingly slap-dash world of plastic toys and pre-fab construction. I had forgotten that I ever told Joe that the big thing was to enjoy what you do. It never seemed to me that he paid much attention to anything I told him, but if he listened to that one, I feel good about it.

—Letter to Jon Wilson (editor of *Wooden Boat* magazine) October 11, 1983; *Letters of E. B. White,* Rev. Ed., p. 669.

* The article by Jon Wilson, about E. B. White's son, Joel White, was published in *Mercedes* magazine.

Worry

If an unhappy childhood is indispensable for a writer, I am ill-equipped: I missed out on all that and was neither deprived nor unloved. It would be inaccurate, however, to say that my childhood was untroubled. The normal fears and worries of every child were in me developed to a high degree; every day was an awesome prospect. I was uneasy about practically everything: the uncertainty of the future, the dark of the attic, the panoply and discipline of school, the transitoriness of life, the mystery of the church and of God, the frailty of the body, the sadness of afternoon, the shadow of sex, the distant challenge of love and marriage, the far-off problem of a livelihood. I brooded about them all, lived with them day by day. Being the youngest in a large family, I was usually in a crowd but often felt lonely and removed. I took to writing early, to assuage my uneasiness and collect my thoughts, and I was a busy writer long before I went into long pants.

—"Mount Vernon," 1976; *Letters of E. B. White,* Rev. Ed., p. I.

I never realized nerves were so odd, but they are. They are the oddest part of the body, no exceptions. Doctors weren't much help, but I found that old phonograph records are miraculous. If you ever bust up from nerves, take frequent shower baths, drink dry sherry in small amounts, spend most of your time with hand tools at a bench, and play old records till there is no wax left in the grooves.

—Letter to Harry Lyford, October 28, 1943; *Letters of E. B. White,*
   Rev. Ed., p. 236.

"Too many things on my mind," said Wilbur.

"Well," said the goose, "that's not *my* trouble. I have nothing at all on my mind, but I've too many things under my behind. Have you ever tried to sleep while sitting on eight eggs?"

"No," replied Wilbur. "I suppose it *is* uncomfortable. How long does it take a goose egg to hatch?"

"Approximately-oximately thirty days, all told," answered the goose. "But I cheat a little. On warm afternoons, I just pull a little straw over the eggs and go out for a walk."

—*Charlotte's Web,* 1952, p. 33.

I am reminded of the advice of my neighbor, "Never worry about your heart till it stops beating."
— *The Elements of Style*, 1959; 2nd Ed., 1972; also to Scott Elledge, August 25, 1982; *Letters of E. B. White*, Rev. Ed., p. 655.

Subtly corrupt people. Vaguely fraudulent people. Talkative people who have nothing to say. Power-hungry people. Creative people with their ear to the ground. People whose names begin with W.
— "E. B. White: Notes and Comment by Author" (on being asked what gives him the willies), interview with Israel Shenker, July 11, 1969; *New York Times*.

Writing and Writers
(see also Literature, Poets and Poetry)

I admire anybody who has the guts to write anything at all.
— "The Art of the Essay, No. 1, E. B. White," interview with George A. Plimpton and Frank H. Crowther, Fall 1969; *Paris Review*, Issue 48.

An Author's Life
My wife, thank God, has never been protective of me, as, I am told, the wives of some writers are. In consequence, the members of my household never pay the slightest attention to my being a writing man—they make all the noise and fuss they want to. If I get sick of it, I have places I can go. A writer who waits for ideal conditions under which to work will die without putting a word on paper.
— "The Art of the Essay, No. 1, E. B. White," interview with George A. Plimpton and Frank H. Crowther, Fall 1969; *Paris Review*, Issue 48.

Thanks for the copy of "Wise Words." I need wise words if anybody ever did. From the number of books you and your husband have had published, I suspect that you will soon have to change the characterization of your lives from "simple living" to "complex living." I have discovered that the life of an author is anything but simple. I have yet to build a house of stone. That's when I'll have to change the characterization of mine.

    —Letter to Mrs. Scott (Helen) Nearing,* December 8, 1980; *Letters of E. B. White*, Rev. Ed., p. 637.

    * Co-author with her husband of *Simple Living*.

A really pure writer is a man like Conrad, who is first of all a mariner; or Isadora Duncan, a dancer; or Ben Franklin, an inventor and statesman; or Hitler, a scamp.

    —"Questionnaire," July 1942; *One Man's Meat*, p. 233.

I suppose a writer, almost by definition, is a person incapable of satisfaction—which is what keeps him at his post. Let us just say that I have tidied up my desk a bit, and flung out a few noisy and ill-timed farewells, like a drunk at a wedding he is enjoying to the hilt and has no intention of leaving.

    —"Foreword," *Second Tree from the Corner*, 1954, p. xiv.

Autobiography

Most writers find the world and themselves practically interchangeable, and in a sense the world dies every time a writer dies, because, if he is any good, he has been wet nurse to humanity during his entire existence and has held earth close around him, like the little obstetrical toad that goes about with a cluster of eggs attached to his legs.

    —"Doomsday," November 17, 1945; *Writings from* The New Yorker, *1925–1976*, pp. 229–230.

Whoever sets pen to paper writes of himself, whether knowingly or not, and this is a book of revelations.
—"Foreword," *Second Tree from the Corner*, 1954, p. xi.

I was interested in your remarks about the writer as poser, because, of course, all writing is both a mask and an unveiling, and the question of honesty is uppermost, particularly in the case of the essayist, who must take his trousers off without showing his genitals. (I got my training in the upper berths of Pullman cars long ago.)
—Letter to Scott Elledge, February 16, 1964; *Letters of E. B. White*, Rev. Ed, p. 470.

Some of them* are tremendously pretentious in the way they're written, tremendously callow, the kind of things that go with youth. But I was observing myself very sharply and very shrewdly. I was never a reader. I was arriving at conclusions almost independently of the entire history of the world. If I sat down to read everything that had been written—I'm a slow reader—I would never have written anything. My joy and my impulse was to get something down on paper myself.
—"E. B. White: Notes and Comment by Author," interview with Israel Shenker, July 11, 1969; *New York Times*.
* White's early journals.

Are my stories true, you ask? No, they are imaginary tales, containing fantastic characters and events. In real life, a family doesn't have a child who looks like a mouse; in real life, a spider doesn't spin words in her web. In real life, a swan doesn't blow a trumpet. But real life is only one kind of life—there is also the life of the imagination. And although my stories are imaginary, I like to think that there is some truth in them, too—truth about the way people and animals feel and think and act.
—"A Letter from E. B. White," ca. 1970s; HarperCollins Children's Books website, Authors & Illustrators page at http://

www.harpercollinschildrens.com/Kids/AuthorsAndIllustra-
tors/AuthorNote.aspx?CId=10499.

Every writer, by the way he uses the language, reveals something of his
spirit, his habits, his capacities, his bias. This is inevitable as well as
enjoyable. All writing is communication; creative writing is communication through revelation—it is the Self escaping into the open. No
writer long remains incognito.

—"An Approach to Style," *The Elements of Style,* 1959; 2nd Ed.,
1972, pp. 59–60.

Communication with the Reader

Of course, it may be that the art of photography and the art of writing
are antithetical. The hope and aim of a word-handler is that he may
communicate a thought or an impression to his reader without the
reader's realizing that he has been dragged through a series of hazard-
ous or grotesque syntactical situations. In photography, the goal seems
to be to prove beyond a doubt that the cameraman, in his great moment of creation, was either hanging by his heels from the rafters or
was wedged under the floor with his lens at a knothole.

—"Peaks in Journalism," July 24, 1937; *Second Tree from the Corner,*
p. 159.

In other words, if a writer succeeds in communicating with a reader,
I think it is simply because he has been trying (with some success) to
get in touch with himself—to clarify the reception...

—Letter to Alison Marks, April 20, 1956; *Letters of E. B. White,*
1st edition only, p. 417.

Duty or Obligation of a Writer

As a writing man, or secretary, I have always felt charged with the safe-keeping of all unexpected items of worldly and unworldly enchant-ment, as though I might be held personally responsible if even a small one were to be lost.

—"The Ring of Time," March 22, 1956; *Points of My Compass,*
p. 52, and *Essays of E. B. White,* p. 143.

It has been ambitious and plucky of me to attempt to describe what is indescribable, and I have failed, as I knew I would. But I have dis-charged my duty to my society; and besides, a writer, like an acrobat, must occasionally try a stunt that is too much for him.

—"The Ring of Time," March 22, 1956; *Points of My Compass,*
p. 55, and *Essays of E. B. White,* p. 145.

I feel that a writer has an obligation to transmit, as best he can, his love of life, his appreciation for the world.

—From an unpublished letter in response to an award from the Laura Ingalls Wilder Foundation, 1970; White Literary LLC archive.

I have always felt that the first duty of a writer was to ascend—to make flights, carrying others along if he could manage it. To do this takes courage, even a certain conceit.

—"The Egg Is All," *New York Times,* December 7, 1971; remarks on receiving the National Medal for Literature.

A writer must reflect and interpret his society, his world; he must also provide inspiration and guidance and challenge. Much writing today strikes me as deprecating, destructive, and angry. There are good reasons for anger, and I have nothing against anger. But I think some writers have lost their sense of proportion, their sense of humor, and their sense of appreciation. I am often mad, but I would hate to be nothing but mad: and I think I would lose what little value I may have as a writer if I were to refuse, as a matter of principle, to accept the warming rays of the sun, and to report them, whenever, and if ever, they happen to strike me. One role of the writer today is to sound the alarm. The environment is disintegrating, the hour is late, and not much is being done.

—"The Art of the Essay, No. I, E. B. White," interview with George A. Plimpton and Frank H. Crowther, Fall 1969; *Paris Review*, Issue 48.

Writing, which is my way of serving, is hard work for me and usually not attended with any joy. It has its satisfactions, but the act of writing is often a pure headache, and I don't kid myself about there being any fun in it.

—Letter to Mary Virginia Parrish, August 29, 1969; *Letters of E. B. White*, Rev. Ed., p. 532.

The Editorial Writer

It is almost impossible to write anything decent using the editorial "we," unless you are the Dionne* family. Anonymity, plus the "we," gives a writer a cloak of dishonesty, and he finds himself going around like a masked reveler at a ball, kissing all the pretty girls.

—Letter to Gustave S. Lobrano, October?, 1934; *Letters of E. B. White*, Rev. Ed., p. 114.

*The Dionne family had quintuplets on May 28, 1934, the first-known quints to survive their infancy.

An editorial page is a fuzzy performance, any way you look at it, since it affects a composite personality with an editorial "we" for a front.

Once in a while we think of ourself as "we," but not often. The word "ourself" is the giveaway—the plural "our," the singular "self," united in a common cause.

　—"Editorial Writers," March 4, 1944; *Writings from* The New Yorker, *1925–1976,* p. 27.

In my job as commentator, I was stuck with the editorial "we," a weasel word suggestive of corporate profundity or institutional consensus. I wanted to write as straight as possible, with no fuzziness.

　—"Introduction," May 1982; *One Man's Meat,* p. xiii.

The Essayist

Satire is a most difficult and subtle form of writing, requiring a kind of natural genius. Any reasonably well-educated person can write in a satirical vein, but try and find one that comes off.

　—"The Art of the Essay, No. I, E. B. White," interview with George A. Plimpton and Frank H. Crowther, Fall 1969; *Paris Review,* Issue 48.

The essayist is a self-liberated man, sustained by the childish belief that everything he thinks about, everything that happens to him, is of general interest.

　—"Foreword," *Essays of E. B. White,* April 1977, p. vii.

The essayist arises in the morning and, if he has work to do, selects his garb from an unusually extensive wardrobe: he can pull on any sort of shirt, be any sort of person, according to his mood or his subject matter—philosopher, scold, jester, raconteur, confidant, pundit, devil's advocate, enthusiast.

　—"Foreword," *Essays of E. B. White,* April 1977, p. vii.

Procrastination

When I want some fun, I don't write, I go sailing.
>   —Letter to Mary Virginia Parrish, August 29, 1969; *Letters of E. B. White*, Rev. Ed., p. 532.

In my own experience I have found that I'm more likely to write when I feel terrible than when I feel great. If you feel good, you don't have to write—you go somewhere and do something pleasant.
>   —Letter to Gerald Nachman, March 15, 1980; *Letters of E. B. White*, Rev. Ed., p. 632.

Writing Advice

Advice to young writers who want to get ahead without any annoying delays: don't write about Man, write about *a* man.
>   —"Some Remarks of Humor," 1941; reprinted in *Essays of E. B. White*, p. 246.

Writing is not an occupation nor is it a profession. Bad writing can be, and often is, an occupation; but I rather agree with the government that writing in the pure sense and in noblest form is neither an occupation or a profession. It is more of an affliction, or just punishment. It is something that raises up on you, as a welt.
>   —"Questionnaire," July 1942; *One Man's Meat*, p. 233.

I think the best writing is often done by persons who are snatching the time from something else—from an occupation, or from a profession, or from a jail term—something that is either burning them up, as religion, or love, or politics, or that is boring them to tears, as prison, or a brokerage house, or an advertising firm.
>   —"Questionnaire" July 1942; *One Man's Meat*, p. 234.

It is our belief that no writer can improve his work until he discards the dulcet notion that the reader is feeble-minded, for writing is an act of faith, not a trick of grammar.

—"Calculating Machine," March 3, 1951; *Second Tree from the Corner*, pp. 166–167.

A pianist achieves a certain tone through the use of his hand, his mind, and his heart. I presume a writer arrives at it in much the same way. I have always tried to say the words and transmit the emotion, if any, and without too much horsing around.

—"E. B. White: Notes and Comment by Author," interview with Israel Shenker, July 11, 1969; *New York Times.*

Prefer the standard to the offbeat.

—"An Approach to Style," *The Elements of Style,* 1959; 2nd Ed., 1972, p. 74.

No one can write decently who is distrustful of the reader's intelligence, or whose attitude is patronizing.

—"An Approach to Style," *The Elements of Style,* 1959; 2nd Ed., 1972, p. 77.

You asked me about writing—how I did it. There is no trick to it. If you like to write and want to write, you write, no matter where you are or what else you are doing or whether anyone pays any heed.

—Letter to Miss R—, September 15, 1973; *Letters of E. B. White,* Rev. Ed., p. 600.

"What's next?" he repeated.

"Writing," cried the scholars.

"Goodness," said Stuart in disgust, "don't you children know how to write yet?"

"Certainly we do!" yelled one and all.

"So much for that, then," said Stuart.
—*Stuart Little*, 1945, p. 90.

A writer should concern himself with whatever absorbs his fancy, stirs his heart, and unlimbers his typewriter....He should tend to lift people up, not lower them down. Writers do not merely reflect and interpret life, they inform and shape life.
—"The Art of the Essay, No. I, E. B. White," interview with George A. Plimpton and Frank H. Crowther, Fall 1969; *Paris Review*, Issue 48.

I am apt to let something simmer for a while in my mind before trying to put it into words. I walk around, straightening pictures on the wall, rugs on the floor—as though not until everything in the world was lined up and perfectly true could anybody reasonably expect me to set a word down on paper.
—"The Art of the Essay, No. I, E. B. White," interview with George A. Plimpton and Frank H. Crowther, Fall 1969; *Paris Review*, Issue 48.

Youth
(see also Aging, Childhood)

Youth, I have no doubt, will always recognize its own frontier and push beyond it by whatever means are at hand. As for me, I've always been glad that mine was a two-track road running across the prairie into the sinking sun, and underneath me a slow-motion roadster

of miraculous design—strong, tremulous, and tireless, from sea to shining sea.
—*Farewell to Model T; From Sea to Shining Sea,* p. 34.

Mother: "It's broccoli, dear."
Child: "I say it's spinach and I say the hell with it."
—Caption for Carl Rose cartoon of a mother and boy at the dinner table, December 8, 1928; *The New Yorker.*

"Go down through the garden, dig up the radishes! Root up everything! Eat grass! Look for corn! Look for oats! Run all over! Skip and dance, jump and prance! Go down through the orchard and stroll in the woods! The world is a wonderful place when you're young."
—"Escape," *Charlotte's Web* (spoken by the goose), 1952, pp. 17–18.

Youth is almost always in deep trouble—of the mind, the heart, the flesh. And as a youth I think I managed to heap myself with more than my share. It took an upheaval of the elements and a job at the lowest level to give me the relief I craved.
—"The Years of Wonder," March 16, 1961; *Points of My Compass,* p. 140, and *Essays of E. B. White,* p. 195.

I'm very sympathetic to what young people say. One day they're defending the flag and the next day they're tearing the ivy off the walls.
—"E. B. White: Notes and Comment by Author," interview with Israel Shenker, July 11, 1969; *New York Times.*

I seldom peddle advice to the young. Most of them seem better informed than I am, and they have their own special problems.
—"E. B. White: Notes and Comment by Author," interview with Israel Shenker, July 11, 1969; *New York Times.*

Parents should adjust to their children by staying young. And by talking to a youngster as though there were no age gap. The gap is real
enough—it is as old as the human race. It is natural that there be a
gap, and not a bad thing, either.

    —"E. B. White: Notes and Comment by Author," interview with
      Israel Shenker, July 11, 1969; *New York Times.*

This is what youth must figure out:
    Girls, love, and living.
    The having, the not having.
    The spending and giving.
And the melancholy time of not knowing.

This is what age must learn about:
    The ABC of dying.
    The going, yet not going,
    The loving and leaving,
And the unbearable knowing and knowing.

    —"Youth and Age" (in its entirety), *Poems and Sketches of E. B. White,*
      1981, p. 99.

SELECT BIBLIOGRAPHY

Primary Sources (chronologically)

Less Than Nothing—or the Life and Times of Sterling Finny. New York, 1927.

The Lady Is Cold; Poems by E. B. White. New York: Harper & Brothers, 1929. Ann Arbor: UMI, 1967.

Is Sex Necessary? Or Why You Feel the Way You Do. By James Thurber and E. B. White. New York: Harper & Brothers, 1929. With new introduction by White, 1950. The Foreword, Chapters 2, 3, 6, 8, and "Answers to Hard Questions," and "A Note on the Drawings in This Book" were written by White; the other parts by Thurber.

Ho-Hum: Newsbreaks from The New Yorker. New York: Farrar & Rinehart, 1931.

Another Ho-Hum. New York: Farrar & Rinehart, 1932.

Alice through the Cellophane. New York: John Day Company, 1933.

Every Day Is Saturday. New York: Harper & Brothers, 1934. Ann Arbor: UMI, 1967.

Farewell to Model T; From Sea to Shining Sea (with Richard Lee Strout, published under the pseudonym Lee Strout White). New York: Putnam's, 1936. New York: Little Bookroom, 2003.

The Fox of Peapack and Other Poems. New York: Harper & Brothers, 1938. Ann Arbor: UMI, 1967.

Quo Vadimus? Or the Case for the Bicycle. New York: Harper & Brothers, 1938. Freeport, NY: Books for Libraries, 1972.

One Man's Meat. New York: Harper & Brothers, 1942; *One Man's Meat, A New and Enlarged Edition.* New York: Harper & Brothers, 1944. New Introduction by E. B. White, 1983.

Stuart Little. New York: Harper & Brothers, 1945.

The Wild Flag: Editorials from The New Yorker *on Federal World Government and Other Matters.* Boston: Houghton Mifflin, 1946. Ann Arbor: UMI, 1967.

Here Is New York. New York: Harper & Brothers, 1949. New York: Warner, 1988. New York: Little Bookroom, 1999.

Charlotte's Web. New York: Harper & Brothers, 1952.

The Second Tree from the Corner. New York: Harper & Brothers, 1954. New Introduction by E. B. White, New York: Harper, 1984.

The Elements of Style by William Strunk Jr. and E. B. White. New York: Macmillan, 1959; Second revision, 1972; Third revision, 1979. Strunk & White and Maira Kalman Illustrated Edition, New York: Penguin, 2005.

The Points of My Compass: Letters from the East, the West, the North, the South. New York: Harper & Row, 1962.

An E. B. White Reader. Edited by William W. Watt and Robert W. Bradford. New York, Harper & Row, 1966.

Trumpet of the Swan. New York: Harper & Row, 1970.

The Letters of E. B. White. Edited by Dorothy Lobrano Guth. New York: Harper & Row, 1976; Revised Edition, edited by Martha White. New York: HarperCollins, 2006.

Essays of E. B. White. New York: Harper & Row, 1977.

Poems and Sketches of E. B. White. New York: Harper & Row, 1981.

E. B. White, Writings from The New Yorker, *1925–1976.* Edited by Rebecca M. Dale. New York: HarperCollins, 1990.

White on White. Audio recording of E. B. White selections, read by Joel White. Maine: Audio Bookshelf, 1996. Maine: River Music, 1996, 1998.

Notes on Our Times. Delray Beach, FL: Levenger Press, 2007.

Books Edited or with Contributions by E. B. White (chronologically)

"Foreword." *The* New Yorker *Album.* Garden City, NY: Doubleday, 1928.

"Foreword." *The Second* New Yorker *Album.* Garden City, NY: Doubleday, 1929.

"Foreword." *The Third* New Yorker *Album.* Garden City, NY: Doubleday, 1930.

The Owl in the Attic. By James Thurber, with an Introduction by E. B. White. New York: Harper & Brothers, 1931.

"I'd Send My Son to Cornell." *Our Cornell,* comp. Raymond F. Howes. Ithaca, NY: Cayuga, 1939, 1947. Reprinted in *The College Years.* Ed. A. C. Spectorsky. New York: Hawthorn, 1958.

A Subtreasury of American Humor. Edited with K. S. White. New York: Coward-McCann, 1941.

Four Freedoms. Edited by E. B. White. Washington, DC: Office of War Information, 1942.

A Basic Chicken Guide for the Small Flock Owner. By Roy E. Jones, with an Introduction by E. B. White. New York: William Morrow, 1944.

The Lives and Times of Archy & Mehitabel. By Don Marquis, with an Introduction by E. B. White. Garden City, NY: Doubleday, 1950.

Spider, Egg, and Microcosm: Three Men and Three Worlds of Science. By Eugene Kinkead, with an Introduction by E. B. White. New York: Knopf, 1955.

"E. B. White." *More Junior Authors.* Edited by Muriel Fuller, with an autobiographical sketch by E. B. White. New York: H. W. Wilson, 1963.

"A Teaching Trinity." *The Teacher.* Edited by Morris Ernst, with a chapter by E. B. White. Englewood Cliffs, NJ: Prentice-Hall, 1967.

Poems for All Occasions. By Howard Cushman, with an Introduction by E. B. White. Privately printed, July, 1973.

Onward and Upward in the Garden. By Katharine S. White, Edited and with an Introduction by E. B. White. New York: Farrar, Straus & Giroux, 1979.

Secondary Sources (chronologically, with a few comments)

Biography

E. B. White. By Edward C. Sampson. New York: Twayne Publishers, 1974.

E. B. White: A Bibliographic Catalogue of Printed Materials at the Department of Rare Books, Cornell University Library. By Katharine Romans Hall. Preface by E. B. White. New York: Garland, 1979. [Everything you wanted to know (but were afraid to ask) about virtually everything White wrote.]

E. B. White: A Biography, By Scott Elledge. New York: Norton, 1984. [White authorized this biography—which took Elledge sixteen years in the making—and corrected early proofs for accuracy.]

Onward and Upward, A Biography of Katharine S. White. By Linda H. Davis. New York, Harper & Row, 1987. [White authorized this biography of his wife published a decade after her death.]

E. B. White, Some Writer. By Beverly Gherman. New York: Atheneum, 1992. [A biography for juvenile readers.]

The Annotated Charlotte's Web. Introduction and Notes by Peter F. Neumeyer. New York: HarperCollins, 1994.

E. B. White, The Elements of a Writer. By Janice Tingum. Minneapolis: Lerner Publications, 1995. [Another biography for juvenile readers.]

Criticism and Reviews

Ingersoll, Ralph. "The New Yorker." *Fortune,* August, 1934.

Thurber, James. "E. B. W." *Saturday Review,* October 15, 1938. Reprinted in *Essay Annual* (1939) and in *The Saturday Review Gallery* (1959). [In a letter to Thurber, mid-October, 1938, White commented: "I opened up the Sat Review and got into one of my wincing moods, ready for a good old-fashioned wince, but I'm damned if I didn't come through in good shape. Why I hardly got even so much as a little teeny squirm out of your piece. I am much obliged (yes terribly much obliged) to you for your warm, courteous, and ept treatment of a rather weak, skinny subject. Only here and there were you far off" (*Letters of E. B. White,* Rev. Ed., p. 173).]

Van Gelder, Robert. "An Interview with Mr. E. B. White, Essayist." *New York Times Book Review,* August 2, 1942. Reprinted in Van Gelder's *Writers and Writing,* New York: Charles Scribner's Sons, 1946.

Kunitz, Stanley J., ed. *Twentieth Century Authors.* New York: H.W. Wilson, 1942.

Trilling, Diana. "Humanity and Humor." *Nation* (August 8, 1942). [A review of *One Man's Meat* by a particularly insightful reviewer.]

Fadiman, Clifton. "In Praise of E. B. White." *New York Times Book Review,* June 10, 1945.

Cowley, Malcolm. "Stuart Little: Or New York through the Eyes of a Mouse." *New York Times Book Review,* October 28, 1945.

Beck, Warren. "E. B. White." *College English,* April, 1946. [White's biographer, Scott Elledge, called this the "best" of the critical essays he considered, but said he tended to prefer the book reviewers over the critical essayists.]

Ingersoll, Ralph. "White Is the World's Best Writer on the World's Most Vital Issue." *PM,* November, 1946. [Ingersoll was reviewing *The Wild Flag* here.]

Warshow, Robert. "Melancholy to the End." *Partisan Review,* 14 (January–February 1947). [An opposing review of *The Wild Flag,* more negative.]

Gibbs, Wolcott. "E. B. White." *Book-of-the-Month Club News,* December, 1949.

Bishop, Morris. "Introduction" in *One Man's Meat* (Harper's Modern Classics). New York: Harper & Brothers, 1950.

Welty, Eudora. "Life in the Barn Was Very Good." *New York Times Book Review,* October 19, 1952. [On *Charlotte's Web,* Eudora Welty said: "As a piece of work it is just about perfect."]

Thurber, James. *The Years with Ross.* Boston: Little, Brown, 1959.

Shenker, Israel. "E. B. White: Notes and Comment by the Author." *New York Times,* July 11, 1969. [This interview, on the occasion of White's seventieth birthday, was written (in large part) by White who responded to a questionnaire that Shenker had sent him. Many quotations from this interview are included in this book, by permission.]

Plimpton, George A., and Frank H. Crowther. "The Art of the Essay, No. I., E. B. White." *Paris Review* Issue 48 (Fall, 1969). [Many quotations from this excellent interview are included in this book, by permission.]

Crowley, James G. "In Quest of E. B. White." *Boston Globe Magazine,* June 30, 1974.

Updike, John. "Remarks on the Occasion of E. B. White Receiving the 1971 National Medal for Literature, 12/2/71." *Picked-Up Pieces.* New York, Alfred A. Knopf, 1975. [E. B. White's wife Katharine White was John Updike's editor for many years at *The New Yorker* and the Whites and Updike remained lifelong friends.]

Franks, Lucinda. "E. B. White Takes on Xerox and Wins." *New York Times,* June 15, 1976. [On the subject of endorsements or advertiser subsidies, to writers or magazines.]

Mitgang, Herbert. "Down East with E. B. White." *New York Times,* November 17, 1976.

Stafford, Jean. "A Green Thumb in a Mass of Clenched Fists." *Saturday Review,* December 11, 1976. [Reviewing *The Letters of E. B. White* (1st edition).]

Updike, John. "Of Beauty and Consternation." *The New Yorker,* December 27, 1976. [Reviewing *Letters of E. B. White* (1st edition) Updike wrote the Foreword to the Revised Edition in 2006.]

Welty, Eudora. "Dateless Virtues." *New York Times Book Review,* September 25, 1977. [Review of *Essays of E. B. White.*]

Mitgang, Herbert. "Behind the Best Sellers: E. B. White." *New York Times Book Review,* November 20, 1977.

INDEX